MW01491449

UNDERSTANDING
LORRIE MOORE

Understanding Contemporary American Literature
Matthew J. Bruccoli, Series Editor

Volumes on

Edward Albee • Sherman Alexie • Nicholson Baker • John Barth
Donald Barthelme • The Beats • The Black Mountain Poets
Robert Bly • T. C. Boyle • Raymond Carver • Fred Chappell
Chicano Literature • Contemporary American Drama
Contemporary American Horror Fiction
Contemporary American Literary Theory
Contemporary American Science Fiction, 1926–1970
Contemporary American Science Fiction, 1970–2000
Contemporary Chicana Literature • Robert Coover • James Dickey
E. L. Doctorow • Rita Dove • John Gardner • George Garrett
John Hawkes • Joseph Heller • Lillian Hellman • Beth Henley
John Irving • Randall Jarrell • Charles Johnson • Adrienne Kennedy
William Kennedy • Jack Kerouac • Jamaica Kincaid
Tony Kushner • Ursula K. Le Guin • Denise Levertov
Bernard Malamud • Bobbie Ann Mason • Jill McCorkle
Carson McCullers • W. S. Merwin • Arthur Miller • Lorrie Moore
Toni Morrison's Fiction • Vladimir Nabokov • Gloria Naylor
Joyce Carol Oates • Tim O'Brien • Flannery O'Connor
Cynthia Ozick • Walker Percy • Katherine Anne Porter
Richard Powers • Reynolds Price • Annie Proulx
Thomas Pynchon • Theodore Roethke • Philip Roth
May Sarton • Hubert Selby, Jr. • Mary Lee Settle • Neil Simon
Isaac Bashevis Singer • Jane Smiley • Gary Snyder
William Stafford • Anne Tyler • Kurt Vonnegut
David Foster Wallace • Robert Penn Warren • James Welch
Eudora Welty • Tennessee Williams • August Wilson • Charles Wright

UNDERSTANDING
LORRIE
MOORE

Alison Kelly

The University of South Carolina Press

Published by the University of South Carolina Press
Columbia, South Carolina 29208

www.sc.edu/uscpress

Manufactured in the United States of America

18 17 16 15 14 13 12 11 10 09   10 9 8 7 6 5 4 3 2 1

Library of Congress Cataloging-in-Publication Data

Kelly, Alison, 1965–
   Understanding Lorrie Moore / Alison Kelly.
      p. cm. — (Understanding contemporary American literature)
   Includes bibliographical references and index.
   ISBN 978-1-57003-823-5 (cloth : alk. paper)
   1. Moore, Lorrie—Criticism and interpretation. I. Title.
   PS3563.O6225Z75 2009
   813'.54—dc22

                                                                     2009003745

Contents

Series Editor's Preface

The volumes of *Understanding Contemporary American Literature* have been planned as guides or companions for students as well as good nonacademic readers. The editor and publisher perceive a need for these volumes because much of the influential contemporary literature makes special demands. Uninitiated readers encounter difficulty in approaching works that depart from the traditional forms and techniques of prose and poetry. Literature relies on conventions, but the conventions keep evolving; new writers form their own conventions—which in time may become familiar. Put simply, *UCAL* provides instruction in how to read certain contemporary writers—identifying and explicating their material, themes, use of language, point of view, structures, symbolism, and responses to experience.

The word *understanding* in the titles was deliberately chosen. Many willing readers lack an adequate understanding of how contemporary literature works; that is, what the author is attempting to express and the means by which it is conveyed. Although the criticism and analysis in the series have been aimed at a level of general accessibility, these introductory volumes are meant to be applied in conjunction with the works they cover. They do not provide a substitute for the works and authors they introduce, but rather prepare the reader for more profitable literary experiences.

M. J. B.

Acknowledgments

I was fortunate to write this book with the support of a fellowship at the Rothermere American Institute, University of Oxford. My thanks to the then director, Professor Paul Giles, for providing this opportunity, to Tim Pottle and Pauline Wyman for practical assistance, and to fellow fellows for their—well—fellowship.

The late Professor Matthew J. Bruccoli of the University of South Carolina commented graciously on draft material, and I wish to record my respectful appreciation of his good offices. At the University of South Carolina Press, James Denton, Karen Beidel, and Jonathan Haupt are among those whose efficient services I gratefully acknowledge.

I had the pleasure of meeting Lorrie Moore in Oxford in May 2008 and subsequently of conducting an e-mail interview with her, excerpts of which are included in these pages.

My research on Moore began at the University of Reading under the supervision of Dr. David Brauner. I am grateful to David for invaluable guidance, both during and since my doctoral studies, and for providing, in his work on Philip Roth and others, a model of good scholarship.

Professor Sue Vice of the University of Sheffield gave me my first book by Lorrie Moore and thus planted the seed that grew into this project. My husband, John Davey, tended and watered it (and me) over a six-year period from germination to fruition, for which I am most affectionately grateful. The book is dedicated to John, our children, and my parents.

CHAPTER 1

Introduction

One of Lorrie Moore's early short stories starts with some discouraging advice for the aspiring writer: "First, try to be something, anything, else. A movie star / astronaut. A movie star / missionary. A movie star / kindergarten teacher. President of the World."[1] The tone of droll irony has since become Moore's trademark: the more painful the experience, the likelier she is to make it the subject of a joke. In "How to Become a Writer," the pain revolves around failure and loneliness, the twin dangers of the would-be writer's life. According to this story, there is about as much chance of succeeding as a writer as there is of becoming a screen idol or world president; in all these endeavors, the young aspirant is liable to "fail miserably"—"miserably" being the operative word.

Moore herself does not appear to have suffered the setbacks in pursuit of a literary calling that "How to Become a Writer" describes. Her potential was indicated in 1976, when at the age of nineteen she won *Seventeen* magazine's fiction prize for a story called "Raspberries." At that time she was an English major at St. Lawrence University in Canton, New York, having won a Regents Scholarship from her high school in Glens Falls, New York. While at St. Lawrence she took creative writing classes and edited the university's literary journal. She was awarded the Paul L. Wolfe Memorial Prize for Literature in 1978 and graduated summa cum laude in English the same year.

Interviewed in 2005 about her early success, Moore attributed it to perseverance, using phrases that suggest doggedness rather than talent: "I just kept going, . . . I could plod along . . . and no one discouraged me." In other youthful pastimes such as ballet and painting, she possessed only moderate gifts and lacked determination, but the desire to write went deeper: "I came to writing out of various sensitivities, plus a love of art and literature, and a capacity for solitude."[2] After graduating she moved to Manhattan and worked for two years as a paralegal, storing up experiences and observations that would later make their way into her fiction but by her own account not accomplishing much writing while she lived in the metropolis: "It was completely inspiring and stimulating and a great place to walk and brainstorm but . . . I couldn't get much actual work done there."[3]

If during this period Moore considered becoming something other than a writer—perhaps, like Francie in "How to Become a Writer," toying with the idea of applying to law school instead—her misgivings did not last long. By 1980 she had enrolled in the master of fine arts program at Cornell, where one of her tutors was Alison Lurie. It was at this point that she became single minded about her writing, giving up the piano, which she had played all her life, in order to save her hands, her mind, and her energies for the typewriter.[4] Publication of her work began in magazines such as *Ms., Fiction International,* and *StoryQuarterly,* and in 1982 she received the A. L. Andrews Prize for three stories in her master's thesis: "What Is Seized," "How to Be an Other Woman," and "The Kid's Guide to Divorce." These, along with "How to Become a Writer" and five others, constituted the collection *Self-Help,* which Alison Lurie's agent, Melanie Jackson, sold to Victoria Wilson at Knopf in 1983, when Moore was twenty-six.

With the appearance of *Self-Help* in 1985, Moore's foothold in American letters was secured. By then, having stayed on as a lecturer at Cornell from 1982 to 1984, she had accepted a position at the University of Wisconsin and moved to Madison. This relocation from the Northeast to the Midwest surfaces repeatedly in her fiction, which alternates between urban and provincial settings and frequently features characters who migrate between "the boonies" and New York.[5] Moore explores the cultures associated with these landscapes, along with her characters' often ambivalent senses of belonging and allegiance, from a perspective that reflects her own shifting identifications with the East and Midwest. As a new resident in Wisconsin she feels she was able to observe it as a "displaced author," offering an outsider's view that was "interesting and at least half-true." More than twenty years on, she says she has lost that detachment and may even have become a midwesterner, "whatever that means. . . . I did root for the Rams in the Super Bowl."[6]

However at home Moore may have become in the Midwest, her fiction preserves an ironic distance from this as from all milieus, holding familiar social practices up to an estranging light. This satirical tendency counterbalances what she has identified as the inevitable loss, over time, of the "freshness and clarity" of a newcomer's vision; she is never so immersed in or assimilated to a particular environment as to lose the power of illuminating what is ridiculous or disturbing in it. In a story first published in 1989, for instance, a sophisticated New York poet takes a visiting fellowship in "the sticks," where she falls in love with a lawyer who describes himself as not at all "literaturery" and likes to go hunting. The poet parodies the predatory machismo of midwestern gun culture, quipping when she tries aiming an unloaded gun, "I can feel the urge coming on to blow away that cutting board"; but she also ridicules the unthinking, automated, costly habits of metropolitan existence, admitting that in preference to dancing, New Yorkers "just wait in line at cash machines."[7]

Moore's adroit pen portraits of places and people reflect her overarching artistic purpose, which she has described as "trying to register the way we, here in America, live."[8] This is an important insight because it underlines her commitment to a national literature—a literature about America and Americans. With storylines revolving largely around personal relationships, Moore's fiction may seem preoccupied with private emotions that are universal in nature: the loves and losses, dreams and disappointments that human beings experience the world over. In subtle ways, however, the individuals in her narratives are placed in the specific context of the United States in the late twentieth or early twenty-first century. American history and politics do not dominate her works, but they are present in telling details that reflect the impact of these larger forces on her characters' lives. For example, Francie in "How to Become a Writer" suffers acutely on behalf of a brother who is crippled in Vietnam. The story is not obviously a Vietnam War story. Only seven sentences explicitly concern this unnamed young veteran, but his injury and traumatization cause Francie a despair that infects her whole existence and is literally unutterable: "There are no words for this. Your typewriter hums. You can find no words."[9]

By these unobtrusive means and on a small scale, Moore anatomizes American society as revealingly in her way as do writers such as John Updike or Tom Wolfe, who place American mores and politics more prominently in the foreground of their work. Born in 1957 Moore belongs to a post–World War II generation that came to political consciousness during the cold war, Vietnam, and Watergate. She was a young adult in the Reagan years and has lived most of her voting, taxpaying life under Republican presidents. Her critical, dissenting stance comes through in the fiction, as does the cultural atmosphere of these decades, with their evolving rock and pop scenes, visual media, slogans, and idioms. Moore has defined the "historical" property of fictional narrative as consisting in the record it provides "of inner and outer": its ability to chronicle both the inner, private lives of characters and the outer, public life of the times in which they take place.[10] Her characters' personal dramas are enacted against a recognizably American backdrop composed of myriad details, allusions, and conversations. Through the accumulation of these individual histories, Moore's fiction captures something of the inexhaustible variety of American lifestyles and experiences—a national diversity that she considers it the writer's duty to record: "In this country there is a great range in the way people live, and this has to be acknowledged and felt by all of us."[11]

In a work published a year after *Self-Help*, a novel called *Anagrams*, Moore explores the variety of American life in an experimental way.[12] The three main characters in the novel reappear in its five sections in shifting guises, their occupations, places of residence, and relationships undergoing transpositions that resemble the reshuffling of letters in the word game alluded to in the title. Moore has attributed these reimaginings to her interest in the unrealized possibilities in every life course—what Robert Frost termed "the roads not taken."[13] By dispensing with certain novelistic conventions, Moore allowed her heroine to sample several lifestyles—as a nightclub singer, literature teacher, or aerobics instructor in Fitchville, USA; a lecturer in art history in California; a femme fatale; or a broken-hearted, unrequited lover. The form, as she puts it, was a response to "the choices people make, the limited choices people have in life, the variations that people can't explore but in fiction perhaps you can explore them."[14] At the time she was writing the novel, Moore was still traveling uncertainly between Madison and Manhattan, and her heroine's unstable identity may also reflect her own somewhat rootless existence in the mid-1980s.

The form of *Anagrams* was not popular with readers and critics at the time—it "got a lot of bad reviews and did terribly"[15]— and has since earned Moore an inaccurate reputation in some quarters as a postmodern writer. Moore includes postmodernists such as Donald Barthelme, Gilbert Sorrentino, and Thomas Pynchon in the long and wide-ranging list of writers she admires,[16] and a degree of postmodern influence is evident in the verbal play throughout her work as well as in the experimental and metafictional qualities of *Anagrams,* but Moore's steadfast commitment to capturing the texture of human life always predominates over any deconstructionist inclinations. "Literature occurs," she says, "when one feels life on the page."[17] In a radio interview in 1999 she elaborated on this commitment to constructing "an accurate record of life and the world": "When I'm in the world of a particular story I'm just recording what would be true about that world and what would be true about the emotional life of that world and what would be true to the physical texture and details and psychological reality of that world."[18]

The emotional and psychological reality of Benna Carpenter's world in *Anagrams* is powerfully constructed and very bleak. Looking back Moore feels that although the novel has redeeming features, it is "chock-full of mistakes of judgment and taste and sensibility." Twenty-six when she began it and twenty-nine when it was published, she was still at an early stage in what she calls "Learning to Write." Her intended theme was "creative remedies" for loss and sorrow, but she ended up producing a meditation on loneliness that bears the imprint of her own "crazy solitude" in her late twenties.[19]

Moore's next book was a novel for nine- to twelve-year-old children, *The Forgotten Helper* (1987).[20] A Christmas story about the friendship between one of Santa's elves and a badly behaved little girl, it is a relatively slight work that was itself virtually forgotten until Yearling Books reissued it in 2002. No other books for children have followed, although Moore disclosed in 2005 that she has written the text for a picture book.[21] If writing *for* children did not have a lasting appeal, however, she has been consistently successful in writing *about* children and childhood. Whether through youthful characters or adult narrators' memories of younger days, Moore has exploited the tension between naïveté and shrewdness in the child's consciousness to estrange and puncture adult conduct. Learning to decode or mimic adults' language, and to measure the gap between their ostensible and their actual motivations, children in Moore's work evolve from innocence to irony. Sometimes in their precocious or cynical understandings, sometimes in their ingenuous *mis*understandings, they point up dissemblings, deceptions, and disappointments. They are translators, interpreters whose constructions and misconstructions have moral value. As Moore put it in her introduction to *The Faber Book of Contemporary Stories about Childhood*, acknowledging the influence of *What Maisie Knew* by Henry James, in the best literature about the adolescent consciousness "knowledge is the story; its rough and specific acquisition is the plot."[22] Most of the stories she selected for the Faber anthology—including pieces by Margaret Atwood, Sandra Cisneros, Louise Erdrich, Ellen Gilchrist, and Alice Munro—revolve, in her words, around "moral occasions—

moments in childhood when something becomes known, something else is tested, some fact steps fiercely forward, some circumstance is discerned or milestone encountered."[23]

If this suggests an association of children with inevitable disillusionment, children in Moore's fiction also have a more affirmative function, as reminders of the powerful human capacity for love. The ardor of youthful friendship and romance, the trust that small children place in their parents, and, above all, the passion that adults feel for their offspring all represent the highest emotions she portrays: conditions of loving and being loved that are tantamount to secular states of grace. The loss or lack of such bonds is a cause of desolation throughout Moore's work and accounts for much of the darkness of her second collection of stories, *Like Life*, which appeared in 1990. In "Places to Look for Your Mind," for example, a mother's emotional and geographical distance from her daughter and her literal loss of a son who left home suddenly as a teenager produce a profound sense of absence and fruitlessness for which nothing can compensate. In another variation on the theme of maternal love, one of the best-known and most frequently anthologized stories in the volume, "You're Ugly, Too," partly concerns a young woman's unfulfilled desire for children.[24] The sense that something is missing, which permeates *Like Life*, here revolves around the protagonist's empty womb—"furnishing and unfurnishing, preparing and shedding," but never conceiving (70). Her desire to become pregnant is cruelly mocked by her body's production of a mysterious and possibly cancerous growth: an organism that in some ways resembles, but is in fact the antithesis of, new life; it is *like* life but abhorrently *not* life. Disease and mortality infect several of these stories as metaphors for the fears and unsatisfied longings that make all the lives portrayed here deficient or defective in some significant, and often devastating, way.

In spite of this overall darkness of tone, *Like Life* was more popular than *Anagrams* and earned a far better critical reception. Six of the eight stories in it had appeared previously in periodicals, and Moore had received fellowships from the National Endowment for the Arts and the Rockefeller Foundation to assist with its completion.[25] Among the distinguishing features of these pieces is the assured and inventive deployment of simile and metaphor, some of them too unconventional for the *New Yorker*, which carried early versions of two stories. Moore recalls that even under the relatively liberal editorship of Robert Gottlieb, who took over from the more conservative William Shawn in 1987, the magazine insisted on excising certain "dangerously odd" figures of speech. In "You're Ugly, Too," for example, it cut the simile "alarm buzzed through her like a low-level tea," which Moore reinstated in revised form for subsequent book publication.[26]

Moore's unexpected images make incongruous connections that open startling, and often humorous, new perspectives. They go hand in hand with the sardonic quips, witty one-liners, and linguistic tricks that have "come to constitute an unmistakable prose style all her own."[27] Commendation of her humor and verbal calisthenics is not universal—for instance, her pervasive puns have been decried as gratuitous and shallow[28]—but her admirers note the alliance in her work between flippancy and deep feeling, humor and pathos.[29] The narrator's observation about the punch line of a joke in "You're Ugly, Too" is applicable to Moore's comedy, which is often "terribly, terribly funny."[30]

In the case of *Like Life*, the tragedy revolves around people's loneliness and susceptibility to harm. Many of the characters in this collection are spiritually destitute: abandoned, cheated, aching for kindness. As a study of the state of American society toward the end of the twentieth century, the volume as a whole presents a dispiriting picture. Like Jay McInerney's *Bright Lights, Big City* (1984) or Tom Wolfe's *Bonfire of the Vanities* (1987), several of the stories focus on New York City as a symbolic locale —a landscape with metonymical significance for the condition of America. The predominant impression Moore's New York fictions create—like those by Tama Janowitz in *Slaves of New York* (1986)—is of a dehumanizing culture: alienating, brutal, corrupt, and contagious. A young English visitor to Manhattan sees it as populated by "Crazy People"; a struggling playwright is driven from his squalid apartment by traffic fumes, sewage, and vermin into a city so violent that a man suffers a brutal beating for shoplifting.[31] The title story takes the trope of diseased city to its limit in a futuristic scenario in which tap water is toxic and the streets are infested with the homeless terminally ill. Precancerous growths on the protagonist's throat and back suggest that in this dystopia the condition of being alive is itself incipiently malignant.[32]

In a post-9/11 context, *Like Life* reads as a chronicle of American malaise centered on a city both dangerous and doomed. The volume contains moments of affirmation and glimpses of beauty that construct New York less as rotten apple and more as "wonderful town,"[33] but with hindsight these passages seem elegiac, as if anticipating the cataclysm that would later so profoundly affect both the symbolic Manhattan skyline and the national psyche. If at the time of *Like Life*'s publication the city had iconic value as the embodiment of national myth, Moore's engagement with that myth is ambivalent: disconcerted, skeptical, sometimes disgusted, but nevertheless susceptible to enchantment. Life in the America she depicts here is usually nightmarish but sometimes dreamlike, invoking the idea of America as a nation founded for the fulfillment of a dream but from a twenty-first-century vantage point also inevitably containing a presentiment of terrorist nightmare. In 1990 *Like Life* served, among other things, as a fictional study of a sick society; just over a decade later its diagnostic significance was intensified by real-life events and it acquired new meaning as a premonitory, fin-de-siècle—or fin-de-millénaire—text.

The novel that followed *Like Life* returns to the concept of America as dream nation, this time using a small-town, upstate New York setting as its representative locale. In place of the metonymical metropolis, here Moore employs an amusement park called Storyland as a metaphor for America—"a place," as its theme song promises, "where . . . your dreams come true."[34] Enigmatically titled *Who Will Run the Frog Hospital?* this novel is primarily concerned with the themes of care, healing, and remedy, but another interest is in the American myth as this is embodied in collective discourses such as history, song lyrics, and shared narratives.

A coming-of-age novel about a girl growing up in a fictional town called Horsehearts, New York, *Who Will Run the Frog Hospital?* punctures culturally powerful myths through their commercialization at Storyland and satirizes the commodification of American history by the local heritage industry. This is America as tourist attraction, where visitors tour reconstructed forts, go for cruises on reproduction paddle steamers, and eat processed food at the Dairy Dreem. The respelling of the word "dream" in the name of this establishment encapsulates the novel's ironical stance.

The teenagers in *Who Will Run the Frog Hospital?* are scornful and cynical critics of mainstream American culture. They mock the older generation's ideals and idioms, flout their regulations, and define themselves as different through clothes, rock music, magazines, sex, cigarettes, and alcohol. If they believe themselves freer and more sophisticated than their parents, teachers, and employers, however, the novel also reveals them as vulnerable and insecure. They suffer physical and emotional harm, get into serious trouble, and experience identity crises. The narrator announces her project of self-invention—"I wanted to be original. I wanted to be *me*!" (49)—but she is hampered in this enterprise by uncertainty about who *she* ideally or authentically is. Retrospective sections of the novel set in Paris when the narrator is middle aged and unhappily married explore her continuing problems in constructing a coherent and reliable narrative of her life. Her temporary exile in France makes her nostalgic for America, but it is for a past and imperfectly remembered version of her homeland that she yearns, as well as for a youth that can never be recaptured.

Critics deemed *Who Will Run the Frog Hospital?* a success in specific respects. There was praise for Moore's handling of passionate youthful friendship, wistful later life, irremediable damage, and unfulfilled desire, as well as for her portraits of early 1970s subculture and America as theme park or heritage site.[35] As in the case of *Anagrams*, however, some reviewers expressed misgivings about the structure of the novel, judging Moore less adept in this genre than as a writer of short stories. Valerie Miner's evaluation in the *Women's Review of Books* captures the gist of these criticisms: "The form of *Who Will Run the Frog Hospital?* is more problematic. With some editing, it would have made a successful novella, but the story is too thin for a novel. Perhaps Moore is really best in the short story form, for in this book she sometimes loses her grip . . . on narrative line."[36] As a matter of fact, material from this novel first reached the public eye in the form of a short story, with publication of the Parisian sections under the title "Paris" in the *New Yorker* in June 1994.[37] The viability of these portions as a self-contained text perhaps explains some readers' dissatisfaction with the novel's overall structure, since the parts set in Paris are very separate, both temporally and formally, from the longer Horsehearts narrative.

Moore's interview comments about the conception and composition of *Who Will Run the Frog Hospital?* suggest that it was always intended as a novel, one in which a story about adolescent "proto-romance" was "set as a memory, . . . within a frame of adult life, in order to give it context and perspective."[38] She holds that, in general, some material is predisposed to the novel form, some to that of the short story: "The nature of the idea determines which form or genre it will be in, the novel having time as both medium and subject, and dealing with something that requires perhaps multiple points of view or technique or a larger social canvas."[39] The different properties of the two forms are questions she comes back to. In her introduction to *The Best American Short Stories 2004,* she says that comparisons of novels and stories are often most insightful when "fashioned as metaphors," and she goes on to propose some figurative descriptions of her own: "A short story is a love affair; a novel is a marriage. A short story is a photograph; a novel is a film."[40] Not surprisingly these definitions imply greater intensity, concentration, and urgency in stories—her comments elsewhere indicating that these qualities characterize the process of composition as well as the material:

> Like many novelists, I can now work by putting in a couple of hours every morning; but short stories require . . . twelve-hour stretches. . . . I have to see the shape of the entire story, . . . which means that I always put at least one twelve-hour

stint in. . . . A novel is a daily labor over a period of years. A novel is a job. . . . But a story can be like a mad, lovely visitor, with whom you spend a rather exciting weekend.[41]

After Moore and her then husband, the Madison attorney Mark Borns, became parents in the mid-1990s, Moore found it less convenient to completely immerse herself in the creation of new stories: "To write a short story, you have to be able to stay up all night. . . . As a mother of a young child . . . it's difficult to write that way."[42] Her adopted son was four years old when her best-selling collection *Birds of America* was published in 1998, but seven of the twelve stories—or early versions of them—had appeared in periodicals before he joined her family.[43] The remaining five came out in the *New Yorker, Granta,* and *Harper's* at the rate of one or two a year, so that although *Birds of America* is a late 1990s publication, its contents were produced during the course of several preceding years.[44]

The title of this collection reflects the range and diversity of its contents. In its fictional taxonomizing of assorted American habits and habitats, *Birds of America* can be seen as an anthropological counterpart to John James Audubon's nineteenth-century ornithological catalog *Birds of North America,* to which Moore acknowledges a specific debt.[45] The species of Americans Moore portrays include indigenous, immigrant, and migrant varieties: native midwesterners, newcomers from other countries, and overseas visitors. Most of the stories are set in the Midwest, but two revolve around foreign travel, one takes the form of a road trip to the South, and another features retired "snowbirds" who relocate by stages to warmer southern states. America's historical and contemporary relations with the rest of the world, especially Europe, are of more prominent interest in conversations, observations, and excursions in this collection than in any of Moore's previous works. In this sense *Birds of America* is Moore's most explicit study of how Americans behave, and have behaved, at home and abroad.

Surprisingly little of the review literature has discussed this collection's historical and political orientation. More attention has been paid to the emotional intensity of many of the stories, especially those featuring ill and jeopardized children; to what John Blades calls "the lyric grace and poetic agility of [Moore's] prose"; and to the subtle, often intertextual deployment of tropes involving birds and other winged creatures. According to Moore the avian imagery occurred by accident, not design: "I realized, when I was writing the last couple of stories, that this bird imagery was just running through the book."[46] She attributes it to the element of "unrest and searching" in many of the storylines. Throughout the volume characters rove from place to place, person to person, either to escape from something in their past or present lives or in search of something: lasting love, security, peace of mind, a sense of belonging. Underlying these quests is a need for meaning, a desire to make moral sense of experiences ranging from war, to accidental infanticide, to terminal illness, to the death of a pet. In most cases no satisfactory, solving explanation is available, but the very endeavor to construct a coherent account has remedial or redemptive value.

The drive to make meaning is reflected in Moore's prose style, with its concentration of wordplay and metaphor. By drawing attention to polyvalency, shifts in signification, and the rich possibilities of connotation and association, the puns, slips of the ear, misconstructions, and figurative descriptions that pervade Moore's fiction replicate her characters' meaning-making enterprises. The elusiveness, indeterminacy, and multiplicity of meaning are inscribed into "the very grammar of her sentences."[47]

Some stories go one step further and incorporate an explicit metafictional commentary on the necessity, and the difficulty, of conferring sense on experience through linguistic expression and narrative shape. The well-known autobiographical story "People Like That Are the Only People Here" is most illustrative of this approach. The protagonist is a female writer whose two-year-old son is diagnosed with cancer, and the story concerns her attempts to write about his traumatic hospitalization even though she feels that his ordeal undermines "the whole conception of 'the story,' of cause and effect, the whole idea that people have a clue as to how the world works."[48] The parallel between her undertaking and Moore's is clear, and the moral is a revalidation of literary representation: even the most arbitrary, incomprehensible events can be transformed into art. "People Like That" is "drawn from life experiences," Moore says, but "it's still fiction . . . it's organized around aesthetic ideas of narrative."[49] In a more general connection she elaborates:

> I'm never writing autobiography. . . . One has to imagine, one has to create (exaggerate, lie, fabricate from whole cloth and patch together from remnants), or the thing will not come alive as art. . . . One takes . . . observations, feelings, memories, anecdotes—whatever—and goes on an imaginative journey with them. What one hopes to do in that journey is to imagine deeply and well and thereby somehow both gather and mine the best stuff of the world.[50]

The popularity of and critical acclaim for *Birds of America* reflect a general consensus that the slices of American life it contains were indeed well and deeply imagined. Three stories from the collection won O. Henry Awards, and since its publication

Moore has been the recipient of numerous prizes and distinctions.[51] Her output of new fiction during the following decade was modest—three stories appeared in the *New Yorker* and are included in *The Collected Stories*[52]—but regular articles in the *New York Review of Books* and the *New York Times* confirmed her status as a respected commentator on American letters and affairs. In a review of Nicholson Baker's controversial novel *Checkpoint,* she characterized the early twenty-first century as "some of the most devastating years of American political history."[53] Opposition to George W. Bush's post-9/11 foreign and domestic policy comes through in both her fiction and nonfiction, but her explicit comments on the role of the writer in such times generally steer clear of specific political pronouncements: "Fiction has the same responsibilities after September 11 that it had before: and that is not to lie. Almost everything in our culture is lying to us—in some way, shape, or form. Fiction still remains as a means of delivering the truth."[54] Similar vocabulary appears in her introduction to *The Best American Short Stories 2004,* where she identifies one of the purposes of fiction as to bring to light "some cultural truth."[55] The nature of that truth may vary according to the background, circumstances, views, and loyalties of the particular writer, but the test of good fiction remains its honesty and integrity: it must spring from "the deep center of a witnessing life and a thoughtful mind."[56]

What, then, to paraphrase a question Moore asks in the review of *Checkpoint,* does a writer in post-9/11 America— "witnessing the world and taking note of [her] own as well as others' perceptions—write?"[57] In Moore's case the answer to date is three political stories and one much more private one. The latter, titled "The Juniper Tree," revisits familiar subject matter—a woman's early death from cancer—within an ironic, humorous framework that also encompasses dream narrative, ghost story, and even fairytale.[58] Its experiments with these genres are somewhat undeveloped, while as a reprise of Moore's signature styles and themes it lacks intensity, straining for intermittent witticisms and ending with a sight gag similar to—but less successful than—visual jokes she has used before. Far more interesting are the war-conscious stories "Debarking" and "Paper Losses" and the 2008 presidential election story "Foes."[59] In the first two of these, Moore portrays the mind-set and language of war as infiltrating her main characters' private lives: violence, belligerence, fear, and distrust permeate international relations and personal relationships alike. To this extent the stories reflect her stated interest in how "the workings of governments and elected officials intrude upon the lives and minds of people who generally feel safe from the immediate effects of such workings"; how "political things"—here ranging from the U.S.-led invasion of Iraq, to Homeland Security, to a cold war–style arms race, to Rwandan and Yugoslavian genocide—"insinuate or enter or otherwise come to call, visit, make themselves known in quiet or not quiet ways."[60] In the story published in the *Guardian* just days before the election of Barack Obama to the U.S. presidency on November 4, 2008, political issues affect characters' lives in decidedly unquiet ways. The main character in "Foes" is a Democrat whose hopes are pinned on Obama for a national route out of war and bankruptcy. At a fund-raiser in Washington, D.C., he locks horns with a Republican fellow diner only to have some of his assumptions about her overturned as he discovers the traumatic impact of twenty-first-century politics on her personally. The story is charged with both anger at eight years' misdirection from the White House and hope of imminent change, but the unexpected twist is a timely warning against discounting the humanity of one's political adversaries.

A popular writer in residence and visiting speaker, in April 2004 Moore was invited to the University of Central Florida, where she talked to English faculty and master of fine arts students dressed in T-shirts printed with a fuzzy duotone image of her face. Typically self-deprecating despite this all-too-visible evidence of adulation, she mentioned that people are constantly discouraging her from writing novels, adding wryly, "I try not to take it personally."[61] Undeterred by the mixed success of her first two endeavors in the form, she devoted ten years to writing a novel to follow *Anagrams* and *Who Will Run the Frog Hospital?* Titled *A Gate at the Stairs*, from portions read in public it appeared to be a first-person narrative from the point of view of a girl raised on a farm by a Jewish mother and a Lutheran father. These mixed religious and cultural influences, along with contrasting environments as the girl ventures forth into America beyond the farm, suggest a novel of self-discovery. An audience member at one of the public readings pronounced the work "very funny and very Lorrie," while at another reading Moore confided that she saw the new novel partly as a "farewell to the book before"—that is, *Birds of America*—and went on to read a lyrical extract about birds in winter.[62] The novel was completed in May 2008, just before Moore traveled to the UK to promote her *Collected Stories*. She was reluctant to talk about it in detail at a question-and-answer session in Oxford, but in the author's note to *The Collected Stories* she attributed its long gestation to "things she called Life and others called Excuses."[63]

CHAPTER 2

Self-Help

Moore started writing the stories in her first published collection, *Self-Help*, toward the end of her two-year sojourn in New York between graduating from St. Lawrence University and enrolling at Cornell.[1] One of them, "Go Like This," was largely finished by the time Moore arrived in Ithaca. Inspired by a documentary about the premeditated suicide of the artist Jo Raman, it describes a terminally ill woman's decision to take her own life rather than wait for cancer to kill her—in other words, to "go" in a way of her choosing.[2] In tackling disease and death and in focusing on the sick woman's relationships with her daughter, husband, and friends, "Go Like This" marks out some of the main territory covered by *Self-Help*. Four of the nine stories concern physical or mental illness, six explore the bonds and tensions between mothers and children, and all portray the strains that circumstance and character impose on sexual love. Moore has summarized her subject matter in these narratives as "feminine emergencies,"[3] which may sound tongue-in-cheek, but underneath the irony there is a literal insight, since the stories in *Self-Help* all deal with female crises of a profound and painful kind.

The title of the collection reflects the idea behind it: to adapt the prolific American self-help literature designed to coach readers in self-fulfilment and good management of careers, love affairs, marriages, and family relationships. Moore's reworking of the genre is ironic and parodic, and much of the putative advice dispensed by her narrators is highly subversive, as when the narrator in "How to Talk to Your Mother" suggests a forthright response to a woman who has been discussing shopping: "Say that you believe shopping for clothes is like masturbation—everyone does it, but it isn't very interesting and therefore should be done alone, in an embarrassed fashion, and never be the topic of party conversation" (89). The comedy adds to the pleasure of reading these fictions, but it also contributes to Moore's serious artistic purposes: mocking the frequently glib precepts in "real" self-help manuals and revealing human vulnerability to, and tendency to cause, the opposite of help—harm.

First-Person Stories

One of the most distinctive features of *Self-Help* is Moore's widespread use of second-person narration. Six of the stories use second-person address in imitation of life-coaching guidebooks, while three are narrated in the first person. "Go Like This" belongs in the latter category, even though the title uses an imperative mode of address to an implied second person and therefore sounds like an instruction directed at the reader and/or a listener within the world of the fiction.

All of the first-person narratives—the other two are "What Is Seized" and "To Fill"—revolve around diseases of women's bodies or minds, their husbands' treachery, and the joys and sorrows involved in motherhood. There are two cancer victims, a suicide and an attempted suicide, and a woman driven to gluttony, compulsive stealing, and violent assault. One of the husbands is destructively cold, two are sexually unfaithful, and one withdraws from his wife after her mastectomies and resorts to lonely masturbation. The complex needs, disappointments, and comforts of mother-child relationships are explored from a variety of perspectives: "What Is Seized" is narrated by the adult daughter of a mistreated and unhappy woman, now deceased; "Go Like This" by a mother whose suicide will take her away from an adolescent daughter; and "To Fill" by a woman thrown off balance by the twin strains of an aging mother and a too-intense attachment to her own young son. At the center of all the stories is an integrated conception of the links between physical, mental, and emotional suffering; physiological and psychic disorders figure variously as symptoms or causes of, or metaphors for, the absence or inadequacy of love.

Also pervading these stories is a preoccupation with language and how it reveals or conceals character and emotion. The cold-hearted man in "What Is Seized" is an amateur actor with a strong singing voice and a talent for verbal "antic[s]" (25)—telling jokes, mimicking accents—but he imbues even his professions of love with a hurtful sharpness, "like tiny daggers, like little needles or safety pins" (43), similes that capture the precise cruelty of his words. The narrator questions crude ideas of truth as good, untruths as bad, showing the unkindness of her father's refusal to tell her mother comforting lies.

The husband in "To Fill" is kinder, linguistically, than the one in "What Is Seized," answering in the negative when the overweight narrator asks whether he thinks she has "a big ass like a bubble" (137). But the narrator knows he no longer finds her desirable and has resumed his relationship with a former mistress, and her witticisms on the subject of sex reveal the insecurity they are intended to disguise. Her husband understands this; he diagnoses the mental fragility underneath her flippancy in a passage that has resonance for wisecracking characters throughout Moore's fiction:

Tom reaches under the covers and clasps my hand. Riva, I'm worried about you. Everything's a joke. You're always flip-flopping words, only listening to the edge of things. It's like you're always, constantly, on the edge.

Life is a pun, I say. It's something that sounds like one thing but also sounds like even means like something else. (157)

Riva's answer makes her typical of Moore's narrators, whose penchant for puns and similes reflects not only a heightened consciousness of connections, similarities, and multiple possible meanings but also their doubts about anything being what it seems to be. Confined to a psychiatric hospital after stabbing Tom for betraying her, Riva is given a cheese pastry by a visitor and jokes about her loss of appetite: "This danish is too sweetish to finish" (161). The puns suggest a quickness of wit undiminished by her nervous breakdown, but they are preceded by a question ("I'm bonkers, aren't I?") that reveals Riva's fears for her sanity and are followed by an entreaty ("Please don't go") that shows her dread of being alone. Here as throughout Moore's fiction, joking is a strategy for dissembling that actually expresses rather than conceals the speaker's suffering and is a means of self-defense that in fact provides no protection against further pain.

"To Fill" is a sad and disturbing story, even though its ending is more positive than the endings of "What Is Seized" and "Go Like This" and is one of only three relatively affirmative endings in *Self-Help* as a whole. The generally unhappy and pessimistic tone of the collection departs conspicuously from the conventions of self-help literature, which is expected to foster optimism and self-belief. In the case of the first-person narratives, generic expectations are further overturned by form: these are not guides or manuals but particular, individual stories. The specific histories they recount do illustrate common human predicaments and offer up universal human truths, but they do not pretend to exemplify desirable conduct or experiences. "Go Like This" offers a case study in voluntary death as release from suffering, but it undermines the idea of suicide as "aesthetic" (73) or "an assertion of life, of self" (72) and shows not how the process fulfills the narrator's vision but how it slips out of her control. She reflects on its failure to proceed as planned in terms that echo the title phrase, "This is not supposed to go like this" (74), pointing up the story's unreliability as a model for the practice of suicide.

No model for sound conduct is offered, either, in "What Is Seized." Lynnie draws a moral from her mother's unhappy life and resolves not only to arm herself against dispassionate men but also to punish them for her father's crimes, but in framing this intention she renounces forgiveness and embraces bitterness —hardly an outcome conducive to her long-term happiness or one that a "real" self-help book would encourage. And while "To Fill" concludes with a tender reunion between Riva and her son, Riva's course of action prior to this, compulsive eating and stealing and finally an attack on her husband with a steak knife, constitutes an *anti*model of how to respond to marital infidelity. Moore's point is that there are no foolproof recipes for a happy and fulfilled life, that happiness comes by chance or a moment of grace and is often as accidental as sorrow is undeserved and arbitrary.

Second-Person Stories

Most of the second-person stories in *Self-Help* are also antimodels, although they all promise to describe *how* to do something

("How to Be an Other Woman," "How," "How to Talk to Your Mother [Notes]," "How to Become a Writer") or announce their status as guides ("The Kid's Guide to Divorce," "Amahl and the Night Visitors: A Guide to the Tenor of Love"). The narratives are constructed along lines familiar from advice columns and self-help books, employing the mock-imperative and predictive as well as the indicative tense: "Meet in expensive beige raincoats" ("How to Be an Other Woman," 3); "He will be a good dancer. He will have perfectly cut hair. He will laugh at your jokes" ("How," 55); "You are great with kids. They love you" ("How to Become a Writer," 120). As it turns out, however, many of these stories describe actions and outcomes that are the antithesis of ideal: a married man's mistress being humiliated and deceived, a woman falling out of love with her boyfriend and feeling guilty for abandoning him, an unsuccessful writer who becomes lonely and depressed, and an orphaned, childless woman who looks not to the future but only to the past.

Moore has described her second-person stories as experiments with a different way of narrating women's experience; she was using both "the idiosyncratic voice of the first [person]" and "an intimate second person address" to "tell particular stories."[4] The experiment spawned many imitators, and she has accepted the credit or blame for an outpouring of second-person narrative among creative-writing students and aspiring writers.[5] In fact there was already a considerable body of American fiction in the second person before the publication of *Self-Help,* spanning at least the century and a half from Nathaniel Hawthorne's brief tale "The Haunted Mind" (1835) to Jay McInerney's acclaimed novel *Bright Lights, Big City* (1984).[6] Literary critics and narrative theorists have analyzed the precise operation of second-person narration in great detail and have advanced numerous hypotheses, in relation to various texts, concerning the exact identity of the narrative "you." The main debate is whether or to what extent the second-person pronoun should be interpreted as objective reference or address, that is, as the narrator talking about or to someone other than him- or herself. Subsidiary questions concern the position of "you" (if other than the narrator) inside and/or outside the text: is "you" a character within the story or an actual or ideal reader? Or does she or he fluctuate between these positions or occupy multiple positions simultaneously?[7]

The only published criticism of *Self-Help* to date to engage with Moore's use of the second person in any depth is James Phelan's article "*Self-Help* for Narratee and Narrative Audience: How 'I'—and 'You'—Read 'How.'"[8] Focusing on the story called "How," Phelan identifies three positions for "you": as the "flesh-and-blood reader" outside the fiction, as someone inside the fiction whose circumstances and experiences the fiction describes ("a narratee-protagonist"), and as someone inside the fiction whose circumstances and experiences differ from those described and who therefore occupies more of an "observer role."[9] The distinctions among these positions of reader, narratee, and observer are unstable, Phelan argues, shifting in accordance to readers' degrees of identification with characterization, plot, and so forth. However, on one point he is clear: it is invalid to identify the "you" with the narrator; the person telling the story is separate, he asserts, from the person to and/or about whom the story is told.

Phelan's insistence on this rigid separation is somewhat at odds with Moore's own comments on her narrative technique, quoted above, which suggest that using second-person narration is her indirect method of recounting subjective experience—in other words, "you" is an experimental guise for "I." Prose fiction quite often shifts between these two pronouns to designate the same narrator. For instance, Susan Minot's story "Lust" relates its heroine's damaging sexual history by moving between the first and second person. Joyce Carol Oates's novel *Middle Age* extends the technique by alternating second-, first-, and third-person perspectives on the experiences of Adam Berendt.[10] Moore herself includes some variation in point of view within a single story in *Self-Help*, when the predominant "I" in "What Is Seized" temporarily becomes "you."

> When your parents divide, you, too, bifurcate. You cleave and bubble and break in two, live two lives, . . .
>
>   And when your mother starts to lose her mind, so do you. You begin to be afraid of people on the street. You see shapes . . . in the wallpaper again like when you were little and sick. (42)

The effect of the change in pronoun is threefold. It reflects the narrator's self-objectification—her sense of being distanced or divided from herself. It suggests a damaging degree of identification with her mother ("You, the daughter, becom[e] the mother, . . . and . . . you have no peace," 43). And it links her particular experiences with those of others in comparable situations, exploiting the generalizing function of "you" without reducing the story's power as an individuated narrative.

One of the most perceptive reviews of *Self-Help* was published by Moore's fellow writer Jay McInerney, who understood how she was using the narrative "you."[11] McInerney's novel *Bright Lights, Big City* uses the same technique, and a passage toward the end reveals the reason for hiding the "I" behind a "you." The protagonist recalls a conversation with his late mother in which he explained his sense of being perpetually a detached observer of himself. "You tried to tell her, as well as you could, what it was like being you. You described the feeling you'd always had of being misplaced, of always standing to one side of yourself, of watching yourself in the world even as you were being in the world, and wondering if this was how everyone felt."[12] Much second-person fiction creates exactly this sense of displaced characters observing their own experiences as if they were happening to someone else. This oblique mode of reference to the self is particularly well suited to narratives about the strains of sexual love. McInerney's novel concerns a character whose self-concept is damaged by sexual experiences, and there are many other instances in American literature, including Sylvia Plath's story "A Day in June," Tama Janowitz's "Sun Poisoning" and "You and the Boss," and Pam Houston's "How to Talk to a Hunter."[13]

"How to Be an Other Woman"

All of Moore's second-person stories in *Self-Help* either touch on or revolve around self-alienation arising from romantic or sexual causes, a case in point being the opening story, "How to Be an Other Woman." Playing on a double meaning of "other woman" (that is, "mistress" or "woman other than oneself"), "How to Be an Other Woman" explores the damaging consequences for the protagonist's sense of identity of becoming involved in an adulterous relationship. The "you" character in the story is named (as Charlene) and individualized, but a simultaneous impression is created of her as a generic misused mistress. This begins in the story's filmic opening, in which Charlene and the future lover, both dressed in raincoats, meet in Fifty-seventh Street "on a pea-soupy night," a generic, clichéd scenario like the beginning of "a detective movie" (3). Physical description is minimal and indirect, mediated through simile and metaphor (he "looks like Robert Culp"; they eye each other, "keen as Basil Rathbone"; they are "spies glancing quickly at watches, . . . collars upturned," 3). Employing appropriately cinematic techniques, the text focuses on individual sounds and visual details (his chuckle and fingernails) and moves in like a camera to offer closeup frames such as lighting a cigarette (3). A passage resembling a shot / reverse-shot sequence cuts from the future lover ("He smiles as he exhales") to Charlene ("returns you the matches, looks at your face") and back to him ("says 'Thanks'").

Despite this visual emphasis there is no information about Charlene's hair or eye color, height, or build. This withholding of a concrete picture of Charlene is connected to the estranging and disorientating effect on her of becoming the man's mistress —an impact represented, again, with reference to shop windows in Manhattan: "In store windows you don't recognize yourself; you are another woman, some crazy interior display lady in glasses stumbling frantic and preoccupied through the mannequins" (5). From Charlene's point of view there is also another "other woman": Patricia, her lover's supposed wife. On the streets of Manhattan, Charlene imagines she sees Patricia everywhere: "Every woman is her" (12). She becomes obsessed with other women, looking furtively at them and then "quickly away, like a woman, some other woman, who is losing her mind" (12). This image reiterates Charlene's position as "other woman" and shows that, with insecurity and sexual jealousy putting pressure even on her sanity, she is no longer really "herself."

With Charlene's increasing consciousness of standing second in her lover's affections and not knowing whether or how to extricate herself comes a diminishing sense of her own identity.

The narrative voice in mock-imperative mode colludes in this crisis, instructing her, after her lover has left her alone in bed, to "wonder who you are" (8). Using a technique that will become one of her trademarks, Moore increases the sense of Charlene's confused identity through the figure of a doppelgänger: a barefoot "blonde woman in barrettes" (3) who first appears in the opening scene, getting off the bus that Charlene, with her future lover, is getting *on*. With her stockinged feet, shoes in hand, this alter ego suggests tarnished, misused femininity, and her reappearance as a wanderer whom Charlene twice encounters at times of crisis in her own love life implies a lost and outcast future state for all ex-mistresses.

"How"

The balance of power in "How to Be an Other Woman" is in the man's favor, but in a companion story in the same collection, "How," the roles are reversed: it is the woman who is dissatisfied and unfaithful, while the man desires long-term commitment and children. The "you" character in this story is not named, implying that she is a typical, representative figure. The listing of several possibilities as regards meeting places, the man's occupation, the protagonist's professional aspirations, and so forth, increases the impression that this specific situation resembles all unequal sexual relationships. Whether in "a week, a month, a year" (55; a refrain repeated three times), the more powerful partner will "feel suffocated" (57) and "think about leaving" (58).

The protagonist's dilemma revolves around the kindest course of action and the most appropriate moment for making a "getaway" (58). Already hampered by a feeling that any season would be the wrong season and guilt stricken by her lover's hurt, reproachful "James Cagney eyes" (57), she becomes still more trapped by the development of "medical unpleasantries" involving his kidneys: "This is no time to leave" (59). Moore's fiction frequently uses refrains to create connections within and between texts. In this story there is a refrain that begins by referring to medical diagnostic procedures: "There is nothing conclusive, just an endless series of tests" (59); "There is never anything conclusive, just an endless series of tests" (60, twice). Subsequently this statement acquires a second frame of reference: the state of the relationship itself, in which also there is "never anything conclusive" (62). For too long there is no parting, no decisive choice between the boyfriend and another man, no guilt-free ending involving the boyfriend's death and funeral (about which the protagonist fantasizes, 61). When finally the protagonist summons the resolve to leave, the refrain comes up again to show how her future is marred by an unidentified malaise: "There will be an endless series of tests" (64). Another reference to the variable time frame ("a week, a month, a year," 64) combines with the word "endless" to create the impression of indefinitely prolonged unhappiness.

A final sentence reflects on this absence of closure both in the protagonist's experience and in the text that narrates it: "One of those endings" (64). Constructing the love affair as banal and unoriginal and reflexively representing the end of the story as refusing conclusiveness or consolation, these four words apparently identify "How" as a generalized account of a hackneyed situation. At the same time, certain lingering images—of the protagonist in a rocking chair in her "strangely deserted" apartment ("Rock. Hush. Breathe") or of her boyfriend whispering "into the black" the words "Have a heart" (63)—portray the protagonist and her lover as individuals in a unique drama and give their story emotional power and depth.

"How" ends, then, on a note of irresolution and sadness. If the woman in this story is more powerful than her counterpart in "How to Be an Other Woman," she is still no happier. The two stories are companion pieces that invite intertextual reading, but the second cannot be interpreted as a straightforward feminist answer to the first; hurting a man is not represented as more rewarding for a woman than being hurt. Taken as a pair, "How to Be an Other Woman" and "How" underline the absence of a satisfactory formula for sexual love and in the process undermine the self-help genre's central claim, that it holds, and can pass on, the key to fulfillment and well-being.

"How to Talk to Your Mother"

Phelan describes the course charted in "How" as "a slow course to nowhere,"[14] a description that applies to most of the stories in the collection. Instead of making progress in their personal lives, Moore's protagonists typically suffer inertia or go downhill, experiencing a deterioration in their close relationships and gradually, as a refrain throughout the volume indicates, losing their minds.[15] In "How to Talk to Your Mother" regression is incorporated into the narrative structure. The story not only illustrates a failure of communication between daughter and mother but also starts with that negative outcome and works backward through the "you" character's life course to trace its stages and origins. The improved communication mentioned in the title is never an achievable ambition, since the protagonist's mother is already dead when the story begins.

"How to Talk to Your Mother" is divided into short sections related in reverse chronological order from 1982 to 1939. Appropriately for a story about talk, there is a sustained focus on speech, the organs of speech, and various other sounds and their sources. The opening finds the narrating voice advising the "you" character, Ginny, to compensate for her mother's long-standing absence by talking to the refrigerator, using words and phrases ("'What? 'Huh?' 'Shush now,'" 85) that she might have addressed to her aging, dying mother or that her mother might have said to her when she was a child. The creaking, groaning sounds made by the refrigerator conjure images of pain and suffering, while the clause "until the final ice block drops from the ceiling of the freezer like something vanquished" (85) serves as a clear metaphor for the mother's death.

In the following section (1981) further references to sound convey the unnatural emptiness of Ginny's life after the death of her mother. The "hum, rush, clack" of kitchen noises initially implies a busy, full existence, but this is undermined by the morbid simile that follows: "The clink of silverware inside the drawer, piled like bones in a mass grave" (85). Compulsively revisiting (in other words, haunting) the Gothic-style, turreted family house outside which her mother is buried, Ginny encounters shades of her childhood in maternal form: "a figure on the porch, an odd apron caught high in the twigs" and, most symbolically, "a voice at the top of those stairs" (86).

Later in the story, but returning in time to the year before the mother's death, the mother's illness is characterized in terms of sound: her voice "husky with phlegm," a "fit of coughing that racks her . . . body like a storm," her "croak," "chokes," and "gasps" (87). Attention is focused, too, on the orifice that produces these sounds, her "open and drying" lips and her mouth that "smells, swells like a grave" standing as a metaphor for her whole diseased and dying body. Continuing the focus on mouths and words, the mother's physical decline is preceded (in sections running backward from 1974 to 1967) by a mental deterioration manifested in demented pronouncements and use of the wrong names.

As the narrative unfolds, the relationship between Ginny and her mother at chronologically earlier points is reflected in the nature of their verbal interactions. When Ginny's father dies of a heart attack, Ginny is required to provide her mother with comfort and reassurance: "For seven straight days say things like: 'I'm sure it'll be okay'" (92). In the years prior to this bereavement Ginny's exchanges with her mother consist of typical arguments about curfews and housework or heavily edited accounts of college life that focus on literature and omit sex. Ginny's childhood, meanwhile, is constructed as a period of fear, loss, and sorrow partly through muteness or quietness: her father is shocked into silence by his experiences during World War II; the five-year-old Ginny becomes separated from her mother in a fruit market and calls for her "softly" (94) or asks timid questions about a dead sibling ("*1943. . . .* Ask her about the baby that died. Cry into her arm," 94).

For the final section, dated 1939, the mock-imperative voice gives way to narrative in the present indicative tense to describe the moment of Ginny's birth—a "sundering of selves" that marks the end of biological unity. In her preverbal infancy, Ginny is unable literally to talk to her mother but is articulate in ways to which her mother is instinctively receptive: "Across the bright and cold, she knows it when you try to talk to her, though this is something you never understand" (95). If the story contains a lesson in mother-daughter communication, it appears to be that the potential for this is greatest before language interferes. At the same time the final clause seems to assign responsibility for the failure in communication from this point onward to Ginny, who never appreciates her mother's readiness to respond.

In addition to failing (in some respects) as a daughter, Ginny has failed to become a mother; she is one among many of

Moore's fictional women whose lack of fulfillment arises partly from never having borne children. Ginny's childlessness is the result of a series of abortions, which in turn are consequences of her failure to find lasting love. She eyes other women's children, dreams about floating babies, and suffers various unspecified "emptinesses" (90), some of which (empty womb, empty house, empty life) can be associated with her terminated pregnancies.[16] The reference to the "baby that died" (94), while primarily denoting her lost sibling, also evokes her own dead babies, and the numerous allusions to ghosts and hauntings suggest that she is visited by the spirits of these unborn children as well as that of her late mother.

The fact that Ginny was born in the year that marked the beginning of World War II seems to predestine her for loss and grief; her personal biography intersects with wider political and social history at an ill-fated juncture. One of Moore's techniques in this story is to intersperse the account of Ginny's life with details of historical events, political developments, and advances in science, technology, and manufacturing that have the double effect of contextualizing and mirroring Ginny's private experiences. Some of these events, such as Kennedy's assassination or Reagan's defeat of Carter in the presidential election, build a picture of the public background to her life and enumerate relatively impersonal regrets and disappointments. Others, including the introduction of disposable diapers (yet another allusion to babies), are freighted with more personal significance for Ginny, subtly evoking her private pain. In particular, the pattern of references to advances in heart surgery serves only secondarily to trace medical progress during Ginny's lifetime. Its primary function is to mirror her emotional experiences by exploiting the dual literal and figurative meanings of the word "heart." Thus the invention in 1963 of "a temporary artificial heart" (91) reflects Ginny's sudden realization of the transience and changeability of human affections; the first transplant of a human heart, in 1967, is associated with her tendency to "confuse" and "mix up" her lovers (90); and in 1982 the first surgical implant of a polyurethane heart heralds the invention of a synthetic, artificial (literal) heart far more robust than Ginny's by now bruised and broken (metaphorical) one.

The reverse chronological structure of "How to Talk to Your Mother" means that the griefs and losses of Ginny's later life seem, narratively, to culminate in World War II, a conflict that looms over the last half-dozen sections of the story. Bald statements such as "Forty thousand people are killed in Nagasaki" (94) encapsulate the adult Ginny's overwhelming consciousness of suffering and mortality. For her six-year-old self in 1945 such statistics were less meaningful, but the damage wrought by war on her father had far more personal impact. Although on his return he tries to play with Ginny in the yard, the specter of death hangs over their forlorn antics, symbolized by "the dead window in the turret, dark as a wound" (94). While Ginny's fruitless attempts to talk to her mother persist until 1978, when the mother dies, verbal communication with her father becomes impossible from the end of the war onward. In 1945 he is "wordless" as he pushes her on the swing; in 1946 his unresponsiveness to a nervous approach by Ginny provokes a row with his wife; and none of the sections of the story between that year and his death in 1959 describes Ginny renewing her rebuffed overtures—she does not try to talk to him again.

"How to Become a Writer"

In "How to Talk to Your Mother," then, a small number of sentences relating to World War II serve to express the impact of historical events on individual people. "How to Become a Writer" conveys the same message in equally unobtrusive ways, briefly describing the consequence of war for a male member of the protagonist's family and therefore indirectly for her. Francie's brother comes home from Vietnam with a mutilated leg and "a permanent smirk nestled into one corner of his mouth" (125) either as a result of a facial injury or as an expression of the cynicism and disgust produced by his experiences. The disfigurement (whether physical or mental in origin) implies impairment of his faculty of speech—a reaction that is replicated in Francie herself, who "can find no words" (124) with which to write about her brother's trauma. Grief about her brother's disability is one of several factors that incapacitate Francie and make her story a case study in how to fail as a writer rather than how to succeed.

Like the three other stories with "how" in their titles, "How to Become a Writer" employs an ironic version of the counseling voice normally characteristic of the "how-to" genre. The tongue-in-cheek stance established in the opening lines (see the introduction to this volume) is paralleled toward the end, when the narrator offers two pieces of last-ditch advice to the struggling writer. The first of these, "Quit classes. Quit jobs. Cash in old savings bonds" (126), urges total dedication to the task of writing, while the second, "Vacuum. Chew cough drops. Keep a folder full of fragments" (126), undermines this by suggesting a variety of distractions and deferral activities. Other mock imperatives in the same vein urge a loss of confidence in the entire enterprise: "Begin to wonder what you do write about. Or if you have anything to say. Or if there is even such a thing as a thing to say" (124).

Like all of the second-person stories in *Self-Help,* "How to Become a Writer" reads simultaneously as a general guide (or antiguide) and as a particular story about a specific fictional individual's experiences. Francie is individualized by eccentric acts such as making anagrams of the former partner's name and using them as the names of the "socially handicapped" characters in stories (121), and the narrative proceeds in a series of specific episodes in which people are named (Mr. Killian, the McMurphys, Uncle Gordon), the bizarre and usually violent storylines of pieces of creative writing are delineated, concretizing details are introduced (for example, that Francie's roommate once dated a violinist), and jokes and wisecracks are quoted word for word ("Plots are for dead people, pore-face," 119; "*Suppose you threw a love affair and nobody came,*" 126). Embedded in the witty, knowing overall narrative are passages in a more personal, intimate vein, like the one describing the "brief, fragile, untested moments of exhilaration" derived from "writing something new, in the middle of the night, armpits damp, heart pounding" (122). Thus again an ironic reworking of "how-to" literature provides an unusual and powerful form for a subjective narrative.

"Amahl and the Night Visitors" and "The Kid's Guide to Divorce"

Moore stays with the "instructional register"[17] in the two stories labeled guides: "Amahl and the Night Visitors: A Guide to the Tenor of Love" and "The Kid's Guide to Divorce." Again alternating between imperative and descriptive prose, these two stories subvert the trajectory and tone of standard self-help guides as they construct engaging accounts of individual fictional subjects' particular experiences. "Amahl and the Night Visitors" returns, as its subtitle indicates, to the theme of romantic love, contributing to *Self-Help*'s multifaceted portrait of sexual insecurity, possessiveness, and suspected infidelity. "The Kid's Guide to Divorce" concerns the role offspring play in mediating between separated parents, as well as the opportunities divorce creates for children to manipulate adults. In focusing on an adolescent's interactions with her mother, it has strong intertextual links to "How to Talk to Your Mother" and "What Is Seized."

The guidance dispensed in "Amahl and the Night Visitors" is not only about the relationship between the "you" character, Trudy, and her boyfriend, Moss. It is also (in tongue-in-cheek vein) about pet care: specifically, how to deal with a cat that wants to go outside. Trudy suspects the cat of inconstancy and promiscuity and tries to confine her to the apartment, a confinement in which the narrating voice conspires: "Though she will want to go, do not let her out the front door" (108). This possessive, imprisoning attitude is paralleled in Trudy's love life: she suspects Moss of having an affair with the woman singing opposite him in a production of Menotti's opera *Amahl and the Night Visitors*, and (at the narrator's urging) confronts him with her evidence: "Tell him you know he didn't have rehearsal tonight" (100). Trudy's treatment of her cat can be read equally as a metaphor for her treatment of Moss, as a symptom of an underlying anxiety that impairs both relationships, and as a factor in the distance between her and Moss (who, hearing her cooing endearments to the animal, "yells from the next room[,] 'Listen to how you talk to that cat,'" 102).

The way in which characters in Moore's fiction talk to one another is always significant. In the case of Trudy and Moss, their growing estrangement is wittily reflected in feigned slips of the ear on Moss's part. Trudy's apologetic preamble to a conversation about their sex life—"Moss, I don't usually like discussing sex"—is comically misinterpreted by him: "I don't like disgusting sex either" (105). When Moss comes home at four in the morning and Trudy accuses him of promiscuity ("There are lots of people in this world, Moss, but you can't be in love with them all") he defends himself as if against a charge of addiction to shopping ("I'm not . . . in love with the mall," 109).

Despite the wordplay and frequent comic interludes with the cat, the mood of this story is somber, especially when Moss leaves and Trudy lets the cat out into the "sweet unknown" (114). In terms of the story's rewriting of the self-help genre this is a significant turning point, because Trudy decides to trust the cat in spite of, not thanks to, the advice dispensed by the narrative voice. The story ends with a suggestion that Trudy's progress as a cat owner may be paralleled by and/or produce a reconciliation with Moss. When he comes back to collect some belongings and discovers that Trudy has released the cat, his assurance that the cat will find her way home ("She'll come back. You'll see," 115) can be read (though not unequivocally) as an undertaking on his part to do the same thing.

Among the sources of Moss's frustration is the relatively low-brow nature of Menotti's written-for-television opera, in which he is playing the "beserk" King Kaspar, as compared with the previous year's production, *La Bohème,* in which his role had been Rodolfo, "the tenor of love" (101). Trudy, by contrast, prefers Menotti to Puccini and likes to hum Dionne Warwick in the shower. This use of cultural references as indexes of character and reflections of personal situations is a technique that pervades Moore's work: her characters repeatedly see themselves and their experiences in the terms set by external cultural representations, such as books, songs, plays, films. A case in point is the comic moment in "Amahl and the Night Visitors" when Trudy asks Moss whether he is having an affair with a sheep because his behavior reminds her of a man in a film who was having an affair with a sheep (100).

Phelan identifies this technique as the invoking of a "common cultural narrative."[18] "The Kid's Guide to Divorce" draws heavily on it. As the "you" character watches television with her divorced mother, frequent references to familiar films and film segments create the impression that the mother and daughter are themselves involved in a stock situation.[19] The mother's prior knowledge of the film they are watching at the beginning of the story leads her to anticipate developments in the plot, and her own reactions to them, before they happen. For example, she wants extra salt on the popcorn because the near-death of a particular character always makes her cry. At the same time the boundary between film world and "real" world (within the fictional framework) sometimes becomes blurred, as when the mother extrapolates from the behavior of the male lead in the film to that of men in general ("I always think he's going to realize faster than he does. . . . Men can be so dense and frustrating," 50) or presses her daughter for opinions of the mummy (in other words, herself) and the werewolf (that is, her ex-husband) in a horror movie. The mother uses the films as pretexts for conversations about her personal relationships—a maneuver that the daughter sees through and rebuffs: "The mummy's just the mummy" (50).

Throughout the story, as the mother and daughter hop channels in search of something to watch, there are references to standard viewing segments. These are couched in the future tense to foreground the story's generalized quality but simultaneously have a descriptive or narrative effect: "There will be a lot of old-fashioned music" (50); "The police will be in the cemetery looking for a monster" (51); "A band with black eyeshadow on will begin playing their guitars" (51). Some of these references denote familiar segments by means of the term "part": the "part where Inger Berman [*sic*] almost dies" (49); the "beginning cartoon part" of the Late, Late Chiller (50). When the same word, "part," occurs in connection with the daughter's recent visit to her father, the textual echo constructs the father's activities as likewise belonging to a culturally familiar narrative—particularly those activities that would upset or displease his ex-wife, namely, allowing the daughter to drink alcohol ("the part about the beer," 52) and introducing her to his new partner ("the part about the lady," 52).

Notwithstanding this emphasis on the typical nature of the scenario it describes, "The Kid's Guide" creates a credible and touching relationship between the girl and her mother. To some extent this is accomplished precisely through traits that are typically teenage (sulking or pestering for a fizzy drink) or maternal (punishing cheekiness or insisting on healthy beverages) and through typical forms of affectionate interaction such as using endearments or cuddling up together on the sofa. The most effective representation of intimacy between them, however, is through more eccentric behavior, when they dance around the living room together "like wild maniacs . . . pogo sticks, . . . space robots" (52).

Conclusion

The denaturalizing similes at the end of "The Kid's Guide to Divorce" offer a clue to Moore's overall enterprise in *Self-Help*. By means of such images, along with an ironic tone, sardonic humor, a focus on human quirks and foibles, and allusions to songs, books, and films, she defamiliarizes the situations and relationships portrayed in the stories, revealing the strangeness they possess for those involved. Already mediated by being set within a parodic self-help framework, the narratives dramatize the main characters' feeling of distance from and lack of control over their own lives—the senses of instability and otherness that mock facile models of life management.

The use of second-person narration in six of these stories intensifies this effect. Instead of recounting experiences as they unfold for "me," the narrators stand apart from themselves, describing and addressing a dramatized other, a displaced "you." To some extent Moore's choice of this contrived narrative mode can be read as a feminist device, since the experiences that dislocate and alienate her female characters can generally be traced back to their gendered identities and their mistreatment at the hands of men.[20] The generalizing connotations of the second-person pronoun add to the impression that these women's sufferings are representative of the sufferings of their sex, and the widespread use of the future tense implies predictability, as if such things are bound to happen.

Bearing in mind the narrator's consciousness of masculine pain in "How," and recalling McInerney's use of the second-person pronoun to express his male narrator's self-estrangement in *Bright Lights, Big City*, however, it is as well to avoid an emphatically feminist interpretation of Moore's aesthetics or subject matter in these stories. She is attuned to the anxieties and disappointments that make women feel they are losing their minds but is aware, too, of the pressures on male identities. If the unnamed lover in "How to Be an Other Woman" and Sam in "What Is Seized" are depicted as selfish and destructive, male characters such as Elliott, Moss, and Tom are more sympathetically portrayed. Given, too, that almost all the stories engage with or touch on the complex bonds between parents and children, it seems appropriate to analyze these stories from a less gendered perspective, reflecting on their power of exploring (in Monika Fludernik's phrase) "troubled relationships" in general.[21]

CHAPTER 3

Anagrams

Getting published was not, for Moore, the long and demoralizing struggle that it is for many new writers. One of her teachers at Cornell put her in touch with an agent, who in turn placed *Self-Help* with a major publisher, Knopf. It was a relatively quick, smooth process in which both talent and good fortune played a hand: "I was lucky to have Joe Bellamy as one of my first writing teachers and Alison Lurie as my thesis advisor at Cornell. I was lucky to be taken on by her young agent, Melanie Jackson. I was lucky to have my first book of stories land in the lap of Vicky Wilson."[1]

In the same year that all this was happening, 1983, Moore started work on her next book, a novel that would appear under the title *Anagrams*. Like *Self-Help*, this work is formally experimental, although the nature of the experiment is different, and as with *Self-Help*, the outcome of the experiment is a work of fiction that extends the literary representation of subjective identity and experience. The stories in *Self-Help* explored the feeling women often have of divided identity—of standing to one side and seeing themselves as some "other woman." *Anagrams* develops this notion by taking a central character, Benna Carpenter, and shuffling the components of her identity (job, place of residence, private life, etc.) to create a series of "other women" who are nevertheless all versions of Benna.

There are five sections in *Anagrams:* "Escape from the Invasion of the Love-Killers," "Strings Too Short to Use," "Yard Sale,"

"Water," and "The Nun of That." Uneven in length—"Water" is 5 pages long, "Escape" 6 pages, "Yard Sale" 14, "Strings" 30, and "The Nun" by far the longest at 162 pages—they can all be read as autonomous texts. None was separately published before the appearance of *Anagrams,* but the first four are reprinted in *The Collected Stories of Lorrie Moore,* lending weight to some critics' categorization of *Anagrams* as a short-story cycle or sequence.

Nevertheless, Moore continues to classify *Anagrams* as a novel, including in her author's note to *The Collected Stories,* where she describes it as "a novel that took as its form a novella not included here and four stories that are."[2] The novella is "The Nun of That," and in an earlier comment on the structure of *Anagrams,* Moore said that various "rearrangements" of that main narrative "visited" her during the writing process: "The reworkings came to me because of my habits as a story writer, obviously. Reworking people and recostuming them, et cetera, is what a writer does, and so even though I was hard at work on my first novel, one part of my brain still wanted to make stories and was using the material from my novel to do that."[3] In other descriptions of *Anagrams,* Moore has employed three-dimensional conceptions in which the shorter fictions orbit "The Nun of That" like satellites or arms on a mobile by Alexander Calder or in which multiple perspectives coexist as in a cubist painting.[4] Conceived in these terms the five narratives in which Benna has various jobs and places of residence may seem like alternative, mutually exclusive versions, and indeed Moore has said that she decided to allow her characters to "do mutually exclusive things."[5] This is why Karen Weekes objects to classifying *Anagrams* as a novel, preferring to call it a short-story cycle whose disjointed form reflects Benna's "broken" identity.[6]

However, Weekes acknowledges that Benna's identity does not remain fragmented but becomes more "cohesive," and that in this sense "*Anagrams* . . . deals quite directly with the creation of the self."[7] Viewed in this light the various episodes in which Benna lives in new places, has different occupations, and is involved in assorted relationships seem to reflect the way individual identity evolves through a life course that may involve trying out various roles and opportunities. Moore takes the idea of a woman serially reinventing herself and replicates it, radically and often comically, in her unusual narrative form, but not at the cost of progression in plot or character. Successive experiences in Benna's life—including her betrayal by Eleanor and Gerard, her love and loss of Darrel, her father's marriage, Gerard's death, and her brother's attempt to seduce her—produce a sense of unfolding biography.

The result is a loosely linear structure that validates the view of *Anagrams* as a novel—or a subcategory of the genre that Maggie Dunn and Ann Morris have termed a "composite novel" and Margot Kelley has dubbed a "novel-in-stories."[8] Feminist critics have argued that narratives of this kind, balancing unity and multiplicity, continuity and discontinuity, are particularly well suited to representing women's experiences because women's identities are plural and processual rather than singular and static: women's self-concepts, on this view, are continually being revised.[9] Certainly what Moore accomplishes in her novel by way of repeatedly rewriting Benna's identity (one of the meanings of the Greek word "anagram" is "writing anew") has parallels in other composite novels or novels-in-stories by women about women, notably Carol Anshaw's *Aquamarine* (1992).[10] However, there are also examples of the genre written by and/or about men—for instance, *The Counterlife* by Philip Roth, which appeared in the same year as *Anagrams*—so a specific link between this particular aesthetic and feminist ideology seems untenable.[11] It may be more helpful to observe that such novels, whatever the gender of their authors and/or main characters, underline the ongoing nature of identity formation, and the individual's sense of multiple possibilities and potentialities, which sometimes slips over into a feeling of self-estrangement.

Moore's use of a linguistic term in the title of this book is no accident. The novel is one of her most obvious explorations of the relationship between language and identity. Whether through anagrams, puns, ironic aphorisms, and other forms of wordplay, or in their responsiveness to poetry and song, the characters show a heightened linguistic sensibility. They use language self-consciously, knowing that it not only expresses but also actively helps constitute who they are and how they relate to others and the wider culture.

"Escape from the Invasion of the Love-Killers"

The focus on language begins in the opening sentence of the first section of *Anagrams*, "Escape from the Invasion of the Love-Killers." This part of the novel is written in the third person and the past tense, with Gerard Maines as the center of consciousness. His reflections on the different ways in which he and Benna use language introduce their respective personalities and the novel's abiding interest in sexual power relations: "Gerard Maines lived across the hall from a woman named Benna, who four minutes into any conversation always managed to say the word *penis*. He was not a prude, but, nonetheless, it made him wince."[12] Gerard's preference for a juvenile sexual vocabulary— "*boo-boo, finky, peenick*"—which is sanitized and made safe by its obscurity, presents him as sensitive and somehow outcast, shrinking from an adult world he doesn't fully understand, in which words can be used as weapons in the way that Benna uses the word "penis."

In "Escape from the Invasion of the Love-Killers" Gerard is Benna's neighbor and unrequited lover, living in an apartment across the hall from hers, where he listens through the party wall for her return from work as a singer in cocktail lounges. One of the novel's main themes is loneliness, and in this section it is Gerard who seems most lonely, a condition that is articulated through a recurrent baseball metaphor. The children to whom he teaches aerobics provide him with rare moments of human connection described as "magical as home runs," while the words "home" and "visitor" on a peeling baseball scoreboard near his apartment seem "to mock him—scoring, underscoring, his own displacement and aloneness" (6).

Continuing the baseball metaphor, Gerard wants to have children in order to "c[o]me home, bec[o]me home" and be "no longer a visitor"—in other words, to assuage his loneliness (6). But Benna challenges his reasoning. If, as he often says, one of his most formative experiences was being cast as a "retard" in a play written and directed by his father (4), doesn't that prove how insecure parents make their children? At this point in the narrative Benna admits to no maternal instincts. As far as she is concerned, a baby is "a reconstituted ham and cheese sandwich. Just a little anagram of you and what you've been eating for nine months" (6–7).

During a scene in which she watches a science fiction film also called *Escape from the Invasion of the Love-Killers*, Benna rejects Gerard's romantic overtures on the grounds that she isn't "feeling sexual" (8). These sentiments identify her with the love-killers in the film, alien beings who "love you and then they kill you." Benna loves Gerard as a friend and is killing him by refusing to marry him. Debarred from sexual intimacy with her, Gerard resorts to the illicit intimacy of eavesdropping when she showers and uses the toilet. To live at such proximity to Benna without being permitted to become close to her emotionally and sexually leaves Gerard's life—and his apartment as metonym for that life—empty.

The deficiencies of home are also, however, strongly associated with Benna, suggesting that her solitude is less of her own choosing, or to her own liking, than she pretends. If Gerard's self-defining narrative is that his father gave him the role of retard, Benna's foundational myth is growing up in a trailer in upstate New York. Arguing that this upbringing was "not like a real family with a house," she excuses herself from having any reasoned or balanced views about family life. "What do I know" (4), she says, and the absence of any question mark indicates that she uses definitive, not interrogative, intonation. Already widowed in her twenties, she makes light of her bereavement through wordplay: "O what a beautiful mourning" (5). But the juxtaposition of this passage with references to her heavy drinking strengthens the impression that her flippancy, like that of Charlene or Riva in *Self-Help*, is a cover for sadness. The final image of Benna in this short first section is not as a sexy night-club singer in a black minidress and rhinestones but as a vulnerable young woman in a ponytail and no makeup, "curled under a blanket on the sofa, watching television" (8).

"Strings Too Short to Use"

In the second part of *Anagrams*, "Strings Too Short to Use," many circumstantial details are reversed. Here it is Gerard, not Benna, who earns a living by providing musical entertainment in cocktail bars (he plays jazz piano), while Benna takes on his earlier role as aerobics instructor, although her students belong to the geriatric, not the pediatric, age group. In "Escape" Benna and Gerard were not lovers; in "Strings" they are. There Gerard was more in love with Benna than she with him, while here it is the other way round. There is also a switch in perspective, with a first-person narrative by Benna balancing the previous account written from Gerard's point of view.

Punning on the typographical and literary meaning of the word "character" and exploiting the resemblance of "word" and "world," Moore has identified the purpose of transpositions like this, which continue throughout the novel: "I was inspired by the idea of an anagram, which is the rearrangement of characters to make a new word. What I did was rearrange characters to make new worlds."[13] The new world created in "Strings" features Gerard as an untrustworthy lover who forsakes Benna, so it is significant that, in his guise as an amateur opera singer, he is performing the role of Aeneas in his own rock version of *Dido and Aeneas*. This detail picks up a passing reference to opera in "Escape" (3) and anticipates Gerard's unrealized aspirations in "The Nun of That." Subtle cross-referencing of this kind throughout the novel creates a complex pattern of interconnections that contributes to its cohesiveness. For readers familiar with Moore's fiction as a whole there are also countless intertextual echoes to other works—in this case, for instance, to the amateur opera singer Moss in "Amahl and the Night Visitors."

Another of these intertextual allusions revolves around a recently discovered lump in Benna's breast. Linking Benna to several cancer sufferers in *Self-Help* (Anna in "What Is Seized," Liz in "Go Like This," Ginny's mother in "How to Talk to Your Mother") and a series of later figures including Zoë in "You're Ugly, Too" and Ruth in "Real Estate," the breast lump serves both as "a focal point for [Benna's] self-pity" and as a source of energy ("a battery").[14] It also provides the basis for a new self-construction founded on biology rather than (as in the case of the trailer upbringing) environment: "I started to think of myself as more than one organism: a symbiotic system, like a rhino and an oxpecker, or a gorgonzola cheese" (10).

The image of Benna's body as host to another organism reprises the theme of motherhood, because unlike her child-averse alter ego in "Escape," Benna now deeply desires a baby. She longs to gestate new life but instead harbors a potentially life-threatening growth; instead of reproducing sexually, her body is rampantly reproducing rogue cells. The fact that Gerard is insufficiently committed to their relationship to want her to become pregnant gives a cruel twist to his words of comfort following the breast-lump diagnosis: "Oh, baby" (10).

Susan Sontag has discussed the "metaphoric connection" in popular discourse between cancer and pregnancy. The disease, she says, is commonly characterized as "a demonic pregnancy," and a cancerous tumor is seen as "alive, a fetus with its own will."[15] In *Anagrams* and elsewhere in Moore's fiction, female characters engage in precisely this kind of "metaphoric thinking" about cancer or suspected cancer, experiencing it as a malevolent invasion by an alien and repugnant organism—an "obscene" mutation of the desired human fetus. To use a term Sontag borrows from immunology, this invader is a "nonself" that exacerbates the self-estrangement from which Moore's protagonists typically already suffer.[16] Benna explicitly articulates this process of alienation from her material self, which reflects her psychic fracturing: "My body became increasingly strange to me. I became very aware of its edges as I peered out from it" (23).

Elsewhere Benna's "metaphoric thinking" about the lump is darkly comic. Situated as it is in the side of the breast, she thinks of it as waiting in the wings (21) or pictures it as a piece of fruit floating in Jell-O (25). Wry wordplay produces the quip that smoking cigarettes with her friend Eleanor is "cysterly" (35). When Benna explains that the lump may just be a temporary blockage of milk ducts, Gerard mishears the phrase as "Milk Duds," and Benna continues the absurd misinterpretation by shouting another variant: "Milk ducks!" (12). Moore has associated slips of the ear with the tensions that arise between people "at really awkward times—times of collision, emergency, surrealism, aftermath, disorientation," so these mishearings also serve to indicate the strained relationship between Gerard and Benna at this point.[17]

The various biological and linguistic perspectives applied to Benna's breast lump reflect a pervasive interest in embodiment in "Strings Too Short to Use." There is a repeated focus on individual body parts: "shoulders, hands, strands of hair" (23), the orange legs and "split-apple face" of a woman in Benna's aerobics class (25), tongues and ears when Benna and Gerard make love (21), Benna's haywire "internal machinery" (21) and the "synchronized plumbing" that links her to Eleanor (31). This tendency to anatomize people, breaking them down into component parts, is the material equivalent of the linguistic device of the anagram, which operates by dismantling words and reconstructing them. Furthermore, some of the specific anagrams in this narrative, such as Benna's unsuccessful attempt to see "*moonscape*" as an anagram of "*menopause*," are connected to corporeal identity. In general Benna's anagrams are disheartened ("*love sick* and *evil sock*," 18), whereas those made by Eleanor (in this part of the novel a heavy drinker who eventually sleeps with Gerard) are more cynical ("*bedroom* and *boredom*," 18).

In a harrowing series of events Benna discovers that she is pregnant, is betrayed by Gerard and Eleanor, has an abortion, and finally leaves Fitchville for New York. The process of re-claiming her possessions from Gerard's apartment creates a final opportunity to focus on component parts. This time they are the properties of her shared life with Gerard—"shoes, dishes, mag-azines, silverware" (35)—and there is pathos in their enumera-tion. Lonely as she is, Benna is conscious of the deficiencies of an isolated state: "Particles were of no value. Up close was of no particular use" (38). This observation, including the pun in "particular," ties in with a television program that Benna watches, which proposes a theory of matter based on "little tiny strings" (26) as an alternative to the prevalent particle-based the-ory. String theory in turn brings us back to the title of this part of the novel. The phrase "strings too short to use" derives from a box in which a lapsed Catholic aunt of Eleanor's stored tail ends of string in all colors. Having specific application to the "ties too short to bind" (32) that tenuously link Eleanor and her aunt to their religion, this metaphor also serves for the weak emotional bonds between people (for example, between Gerard and Benna or Benna and Eleanor) that lie broken at the end of this section.

"Yard Sale"

If there is a focus on components in "Strings Too Short to Use," it is replicated in the structure of *Anagrams* as a whole, with each part isolating and developing aspects of those preceding and following it, producing recurring situations and details along with verbal echoes and repeated refrains. To borrow a term used by Debra Shostak in her study of Philip Roth, the repeated elements are often "counterimagined," that is, re-pre-sented in some contrasting or oppositional way.[18]

"Strings" ends with Benna severing her ties to Gerard and Eleanor and moving away. The "countering proposition" that is explored in the next section, "Yard Sale," is that it is Gerard, not Benna, who is leaving.[19] The resulting fictional scenario revolves around a yard sale that Gerard and Benna hold to dispose of possessions that neither of them requires. This recirculation of goods is explicitly equated to the transfer of feelings: Benna and Gerard are "liquidating [their] affections, trading [their] lives in for cash" (40). As the first-person narrative from Benna's point of view makes clear, however, it is primarily Gerard who is "getting rid quick" (51). In six future-tense passages within the mainly present-tense narrative, Benna foresees that, once at law school in California, Gerard will gradually end their relationship, writing to her less frequently, using deceitful "lawyerly" discourse, and employing euphemisms intended to conceal the fact that he is dating other women.

The impression of the female sex as emotionally vulnerable is reflected in three figures that can be interpreted as projections or manifestations of Benna's insecurity. The first is an image of her future self as a distressed woman running out on to the street in her pajamas (51), reviving the Benna in "Strings" who ran outside in her nightclothes under the strain of Gerard's absence from home (23). The second is a ten-year-old girl, perhaps the ghost of Benna's past self, who buys an item from Benna's stall, whispers her thanks in a "small voice" and walks away with "tiny steps" (52). The third is a customer whose perfect feminine beauty seems to mock Benna's own sexual identity as an absurd impostor merely "prancing around, masquerading as a woman" (48). Together these imagined or briefly encountered females reflect Benna's consciousness of alternative forms of feminine identity and add a further layer to the text's multiple reinventions.

Another version of womanhood is represented by Benna's friend Eleanor, who appears in "Yard Sale" in the guise of a robust, rapidly adjusting person who knows "how to transact, how to dispose" (40). Preparing to move with her husband to Fort Queen Anne in New York, Eleanor gatecrashes Benna's and Gerard's yard sale and tries to sell a miscellany of worthless items, the most outrageous of which is a piece of all-in-one underwear stained in the crotch with menstrual blood. This garment functions in the text in a number of ways. It is the source of one of the most drily humorous lines in the novel, when Gerard pretends to wonder why no one seems interested in buying it: "Maybe they think it's stained" (47). It is also a grotesque embodiment of femininity, hanging in a tree like the limbless and decapitated torso of a woman. It is an emblem of menstruation —in Benna's words, "a menstrual eye bearing down on me" (46) —and it symbolizes female susceptibility to bodily harm, since the stain resembles a bruise.

"Water"

Women's gendered identity is one of the main themes in *Anagrams,* particularly in relation to maternity and sexual love. Moore's sustained focus on Benna's most intimate yearnings— for lasting love, for children—brings Benna alive as a credible character even though she is also very conspicuously an artful construct, repeatedly refabricated. In the fourth part of the novel, "Water," women's desires and disappointments are explored both directly, through Benna's own experiences, and indirectly, through the "real-life" artist Mary Cassatt.

"Water" develops from the final flash forward in "Yard Sale," which speculates about a new life for Benna in which local children play on her porch and ask her why she has no children of her own. In "Water," Benna lives in California, has a house with a porch on which neighboring children play, and is still childless. Now cast as a university teacher of art history, Benna specializes in the American painter Mary Cassatt—a reference back to "Strings Too Short to Use," in which one of Cassatt's mother-and-child portraits features as an emblem of maternal love. Benna's theory of Cassatt is that, childless herself, she created babies with paint—a compensatory strategy that anticipates Benna's invention of a child in "The Nun of That." Cassatt's lack of confidence about her sexual identity ("woman Mary Cassatt, who believed herself no woman at all," 58) recalls Benna's anxieties in "Yard Sale." Meanwhile the unrooted nature of Cassatt's existence ("expatriate . . . weary and traveling," imagining "homes for herself in her work," 58) mirrors the roving and changing identities created for Benna in Moore's novel.

The new situation presented in "Water" counterimagines the one in "Yard Sale" by representing Benna, rather than Gerard, as the character who has made the long drive west to California. The focus on objects, goods, and commodities that was prominent in "Yard Sale" recurs here, but this time with an emphasis on acquisition and accumulation rather than disposal. While in "Yard Sale" Benna was in the process of casting off her potted plants, in "Water" she muses that her new office "could use some" (55). Gerard, cast in this narrative as a graduate student working as Benna's teaching assistant, resentfully itemizes the perks of Benna's superior status that he envies: "free pencils, department stationery, an office with a view" (56). When, during a telephone conversation, Gerard speaks aside in "a patient, Dad voice" (59), however, it transpires that he possesses the one thing Benna most desires: a child.

"The Nun of That"

In a fit of wishful thinking, Benna in "Water" speculates that Gerard may not really be a father but may have invented "an imaginary daughter" instead (59). She also observes that her friend Eleanor, with whom she keeps up an unsatisfactory correspondence, "has begun to seem more imagined than real" (57). These are not the first references in *Anagrams* to an imaginary character; in "Strings" Eleanor creates for Benna a fictional model husband named Perry. But the allusions to an invented daughter and to Eleanor as seeming illusory are important because they anticipate developments in the final section of the novel, in which Benna invents for herself an imaginary friend (Eleanor) and an imaginary daughter named (after Benna's dead husband) George.

Giving a new twist to an occupation assigned to Gerard in "Escape" and to Benna in "Strings," the imaginary Eleanor is here a junior instructor in physical fitness at Fitchville Community College, teaching her subject from a chair because she is overweight and smokes. In making her weight problem a defining condition of her existence, this fiction-within-a-fiction builds on earlier references to Eleanor's weight, especially in a passage at the end of "Strings," when Benna associates Eleanor with the elephants she has seen in a television program (37). The job as a fitness instructor also positions Eleanor as a foil to Benna, who teaches an intellectual rather than a physical subject: poetry. Like Benna, Eleanor started but abandoned a graduate thesis and worked as a legal secretary in New York before moving to Fitchville. Since Eleanor's status within this section is as a figment of Benna's imagination (punningly described as "a very heavily made-up woman," 204), these identical biographical details create the impression that Benna has consciously or unconsciously constructed Eleanor as her counterpart or alter ego.

Benna's conscious or unconscious purposes in inventing Georgianne are complicated. Partly a substitute for a niece called Annie whom Benna never sees (148), partly a reincarnation of the dead husband after whom she is named, and partly a resurrection of Benna herself as a child, George functions primarily as a surrogate for the children Benna does not have. Occasionally Benna marvels at the otherworldly beauty of George in lyrical terms that both mimic the hyperbole often used by parents and serve as a reminder that George is unreal, an apparition: "To me, she is like an angel, a beautiful child ghost" (105). More commonly the imagined scenes between Benna and George are characterized by relaxed and playful affection demonstrated largely through physical gestures, song, dance, laughter, wordplay, and a private language consisting mainly of nonsensical made-up words expressing love. In her review of *Anagrams,* Carol Hill assigned most of its "power and impact" to the relationship between Benna and George, locating the center of this power in words: "Benna loves Georgianne intensely, and in this love, which is sustained only by words, we discover how much this novel is about language, about the power of sounds."[20]

This part of the novel is laced with explicit reflections on language, some of which affirm its creative potential—"Words are all you need for love—you say them and then just for the hell of it your heart rises and spills over into them" (149)—while others warn of its unreliability: "Meaning, if it existed at all, was unstable and could not survive the slightest reshuffling of letters" (131). As a young child, Benna may have believed that it was all right for words or phrases to be almost correct, but as an adult she realizes that language has to be used accurately: "pears" are not "pearls," "Satan" is not the same figure as "Santa," and "*igloo, eyelid glue, isle of ewe*" do not convey the same meaning as "I love you" (131).

As this last example illustrates, critics who complain that the "compulsive" playing with words in this novel keeps the reader "at arm's length from Benna and her problems" are missing the thematic relevance of the language games.[21] Words are manipulated, not gratuitously or in mere show of cleverness, but in ways that tie in with Moore's interests, namely, love, loss, loneliness, childlessness, and the search for a stable sense of self. Thus, for example, the frequent misnaming of Benna as "Donna," including by her future stepmother, seems to undermine the solidity of Benna's identity, suggesting that Benna could easily have been—or might at any time still become—Donna instead of Benna. Acknowledging a withheld side of herself so "dark" that if given voice it would "terrify" (111), she identifies with an autistic seventeen-year-old girl called Donna on a television talk show: "It's as if I know the girl. She almost has my name, and I bet we know things about each other. . . . I have been her" (110–11).

"The Nun of That" connects Benna's changeable identity to nervous collapse or mental breakdown. A sense of split personality is created by switches from the first to the third person, depending whether the narrative is concerned with Benna's private or professional life. In the classroom she becomes "the teacher," attempting an enactment of authority by marching round the room and shouting. The performance is at best an imitation: she behaves "like a teacher, like someone who knows things" (123). The fraudulence and futility of this imposture are reflected in her feeling that she has no access to an appropriate pedagogic discourse—that the language of the classroom is exhausted: "She had nothing to say to them. She had nothing to say and ended the class early" (136).

Benna's unstable mental and emotional state is symbolized in numerous motifs running through "The Nun of That." A steadily worsening crack in the wall of her house, caused by voracious ants (carpenter ants) that share her name, reflects her gradual personal breakdown and the disintegration of her life. This crack is duplicated in a scribble made in black felt pen on a print of Auguste Renoir's 1878 painting *Madame Georges Charpentier and Her Children*. Perceiving a parallel between this black line and the fissure in her wall, Benna notices how they keep pace with one another: as the crack lengthens, more scribbling appears on Madame Charpentier's throat, face, and breasts. If the portrait of Mrs. Carpenter with her family and their pet initially stands as a wish fulfillment, the defacing suggests both the destruction of the dream and progressive damage to or erasure of Benna's identity.

A further motif suggesting madness is Benna's repeated vision of a woman in the street dressed in nightclothes—an apparition with links to Benna's nighttime dashes outside in "Strings" and "Yard Sale." The status of this woman—as a figment of Benna's imagination? a projection of herself? perhaps even a *reflection* of herself, waving back at her in the window?—is impossible to pin down in a text so populated with imaginary characters and alter egos. The symbolic significance of night attire, the insomnia that is symptomatic of Benna's nervous breakdown, and a general mood of yearning and grieving are all encapsulated, however, in a couplet that wittily adapts François Villon's lament for lost beauty, "Mais où sont les neiges d'antan?" in "Ballade des dames du temps jadis": "Oh, where is the snooze of yesteryear? / Where are the negligées downtown?" (138). To dismiss this translation as one of Benna's "terrible jokes and puns" is to overlook the allusion to Villon, the elegiac note, and the poignancy of Benna's need for the balm of sleep.[22]

Loss is the defining experience of *Anagrams*, and as Benna says, the loss is often of "things you never had to begin with" (208). This is exemplified in both of Benna's love affairs in "The Nun of That"—with Gerard, here a part-time carpet salesman and jazz pianist aiming to become an opera singer, and with her student Darrel. Benna is drawn to Gerard for his confused syntax. Her affection for him is reflected in archaic, poetic language ("I liked him much," 98) and the melancholy observation "Life is sad. . . . Here is someone" that becomes this narrative's refrain. But they are never fully lovers, and after his death it comes as a surprise to learn that he was very much in love with her. In this relationship she loses an ardent lover she didn't know she had, and he is separated by death from a woman he never fully possessed.

In the case of the "black Vietnam vet student Darrel who wanted to be a dentist" (90), obstacles to fully realized love include differences in race, age, status, and personal history, along with an imbalance in feelings. Full of "moral anger" (89), Darrel resists the constructions of his identity that he believes Benna wants to impose. When he tells her that a scar on his leg originates in a childhood cycling accident rather than the Vietnam War, he charges her with being disappointed that it doesn't contribute to a picture of him as wounded veteran: "I know what it is you want me to be" (164). The failures in understanding and ultimately love between them are reflected in scenes involving composition exercises using a verse form known as the sestina. Tying in with the novel's pervasive interest in anagrams and other rearrangements, this form features the same six end words in each stanza, but in a different order each time, following a fixed pattern. In one composition exercise Benna writes on the board seven end words all connected to her personal situation: "*race, white, erotics, lost, need, love, leave*" (157). When Darrel points out that there is one too many, she erases the word "white," a decision that implies that the dispensable element in the interracial love affair between her and Darrel is herself. At the end of the relationship the sestina exercise is recalled in six words that together form an uncompromising statement of finality: "Here are the end words: *so, this, is, what, we, are*" (196).

Benna's other losses of people she never had in the first place involve Georgianne and Eleanor. When she admits her fabrications to Gerard, he is uncomprehending. "You made up an *imaginary* daughter?" he cries, and Benna's answer that she has made up "a *real* daughter" acknowledges the complexity of fictions within fictions: inventing an imaginary one would "get too abstract" (203). Shortly after this Benna relinquishes the fiction of George's existence. Her imaginary friendship with Eleanor also appears to suffer by her disclosure to Gerard. Like a former friend who is now avoiding her, Eleanor "seems to have become unavailable" (206)—unavailable, that is, to Benna's imagination.

Under the weight of all these losses, Benna's composure crumbles (recalling Eleanor's deliberate malapropism, "I just hate it when I lose my composer," 65). This is signaled by a turn to third-person narration, which produces a sense that Benna has become distanced from herself. When the third person was applied only to Benna's public persona as "the teacher," the implication was that only that part of her was removed from her authentic self. The extension of this mode of narration to her private identity strongly suggests self-estrangement.

Benna's journey by Greyhound bus to New York enacts this displacement from her life as she has known it, and in the alienating environment of the New York subway she wills the complete erasure of her identity: "She would rather be someone, anyone, else" (217). The brother who has featured indirectly in previous parts of the novel now participates in the action, when she stays overnight with him in his dingy apartment. Unfortunately, he is too inarticulate, and is himself too unhappy and outcast, to comfort her in her losses. When she tells him about Gerard's death he responds with a whistle and, later, two words of inane commiseration: "It's rough" (222). Moore draws attention to his incompetence with words by focusing on the other things that emanate from his mouth: a smell "of cigarettes and small, yellowing teeth" (219), his breath when he clasps Benna in a clumsy hug (220), an after-dinner belch (222), and "his largeness and breathing still close" (225) after he has made an incestuous pass at her and she has fled to bed. Even as Benna leaves for the airport the following morning, it is an emission from her brother's lips that constitutes her final image of him: "His breath floated out into the wintry morning in puffs" (226).

This depressing and scary encounter with Louis triggers a resort, again, to the soothing power of the imagination. In the short fifth part of "The Nun of That" Benna's arrival in New York is reenacted, this time by train into Grand Central rather than by Greyhound into Port Authority. George is resurrected as Benna's imaginary daughter, here accompanying her on a trip (much discussed between them earlier in the narrative) to the fictional Caribbean island of Beruba. George is, in Benna's words, "a gift I have given myself, a lozenge of pretend" (228), and it is in this recourse to make-believe as a salve for loneliness that the power of the fiction within the fiction lies.

Conclusion

The experimental narrative form of *Anagrams* accomplishes two main ends. First, it reflects the sense of fluid and multifaceted identity that Moore identifies as widespread among human beings, perhaps particularly women. Second, it dramatizes the literary enterprise itself, the very process of making fiction: "I believed the novel to be a messy expression of that mysterious banality 'the creative process'—not unlike life, I suppose."[23]

For all the reshufflings of the components of her life in this "narrative acrostic,"[24] Benna retains an essentially consistent nature: funny, affectionate, unsure of herself, uncertain of others, and lonely—sometimes to the point of madness. Karen Weekes has neatly summarized this unchanging core of Benna,[25] but the most eloquent description comes from Benna herself:

> Sometimes as I'm drifting toward sleep, in the beginnings of that dissolution, I wonder where I am, when this is, and realize that at these moments I could be anywhere, any time, for all I know: eight and napping in the trailer, my broken arm in a cast, or thirteen at night clutching a pillow to my neck, or twenty in the arms of my boyfriend, or twenty-seven in the arms of my husband, or thirty-three next to my imaginary daughter; at every place in the whole spinning shape that is my life, when I am falling asleep, I am the same person, the identical awareness, the same fuzzball of mind, the same muck of nerves, all along the line. (105)

CHAPTER 4

Like Life

Critical reception of *Anagrams* was disappointing—to the point where the author "had to stop reading" the reviews: "I just couldn't take it anymore"[1]—but Moore now had two major books to her name, under a well-known and highly respected imprint, and she was still less than thirty years old. She was being linked with other rising stars in the literary firmament, including Ann Beattie, Amy Hempel, Jay McInerney, and David Leavitt, and if one critic discussed Moore's fiction alongside Leavitt's only to find both afflicted with chronic "tristesse," another compared Moore favorably with Leavitt and others in their generation: "She is . . . a fine writer [who] does with apparent ease what so few of her contemporaries seem able to do: She individualizes her characters so that each is clearly and understandably unhappy in his or . . . mostly her own way."[2]

A future as a writer, combined with her position at the University of Wisconsin, now seemed a reliable prospect, though Moore says she never took this for granted and was surprised at being given the opportunity to write and teach for a living: "I continued to walk through the doors that looked like they were open."[3] *Anagrams* was quickly followed by a work usually classified as juvenilia, her Christmas story *The Forgotten Helper,* featuring a bad-tempered elf and a naughty little girl.[4] With main characters who are both misfits and outcasts, the story reflects Moore's ongoing interest in those who, by contrariness or quirk of nature, are excluded from the conformist mainstream of their society.

In the stories Moore produced in the late 1980s, and which would be collected in her next book, *Like Life*, this sense of marginalization is common to all the main characters, whether they live in New York or the Midwest.[5] All eight stories portray men and women who feel out of place in some long-term or temporary environment, plagued by the suspicion or conviction that they do not belong. Journeys from one state or country to another dramatize this feeling in "Two Boys," "Joy," "You're Ugly, Too," "Places to Look for Your Mind," and "The Jewish Hunter," while in "Vissi d'Arte" and "Like Life" the alien quality of the protagonists' surroundings (respectively, Manhattan and Brooklyn) is not just a matter of perception but takes material form in dereliction, pollution, filth, disease, and decay. The shortest piece in the volume, "Starving Again," is less explicit about where the characters live; a passing reference to Brooklyn is the only clue. However, Mave's sense of being in the wrong place for her lunch date with Dennis—"This is not a restaurant. Restaurants serve different things from this" (145)—is a clear metaphor for the wider dislocation in both of their lives.

Throughout *Like Life*, then, deficiencies of place, and of characters' relationships to place, stand for the larger shortcomings of their lives as a whole. It is not just *where* they are but who and what they are that makes these women and men unhappy. Reviewing the collection for the *New York Times*, Stephen McCauley writes, "Almost all of the people in *Like Life* seem isolated, as if some essential connection between head and body has been severed, leaving them lost, a little aimless, besieged by doubts about the courses their lives have taken."[6] Janet Raiffa makes a very similar observation: "The characters in *Like Life* share disbelief in what their lives have become and a terror of how they have lost control of their fate."[7] Repeatedly in *Like Life* characters regard their lives objectively, like discrete entities that can be appraised from a distance—defined, anatomized, found wanting. "My life is very strange," says a bewildered young woman in "Two Boys" (10), while the wary protagonist of "Joy" thinks anxiously, "You could look out at your life and no longer recognize it" (50). An extension of this reification of life is its personification—a device that conveys characters' loss of control over, disappointment with, and estrangement from their own experiences:

How did one get here? How did one's eye-patched, rot-toothed life lead one along so cruelly, like a trick, to the middle of the sea? ("Two Boys," 18)

His life seemed to be untacking itself, lying loose about him like a blouse. A life could do that. ("Places to Look for Your Mind," 109)

As these examples illustrate, Moore continues in this collection to make widespread and inventive use of simile. In the sixteen-page story "Two Boys" alone, some twenty-seven similes lead up to the closing image, "like a moonward thought" (19). Metaphorical constructions are also used in conspicuous concentration—for instance, in "Starving Again," which contains a memorable metaphor for telephone utterances as air passengers ("You saw them off at the airport but never knew whether there was anyone there to greet them when they got off the plane," 142) as well as some eight structures that link vehicle and tenor with the word "of" (for instance, "the hide-and-seek of the heart," "the disastrous cupcake of it [a face]," 142). All the stories in *Like Life* are written in the limited third person, using free indirect narration to evoke characters' inner lives. The similes and metaphors therefore come across as the characters' similes and metaphors, not Moore's; they seem the products of what Mave in "Starving Again" might call these slightly un-hinged people's "blazing minds" (145). Underlying all these fig-ures of speech is a preoccupation with capturing the essence of people and things, as if by describing the world around them, the characters hope to get their bearings in it and increase their purchase on it. Ironically the effect of these often bizarre com-parisons is to communicate the characters' disorientation and eccentricity, as when Mary in "Two Boys" thinks of "the hot lunch of him [a boyfriend]" and "life barking at the bottom [of a tree] like a dog" (8), or when Mave compares love to "the rest rooms at the Ziegfeld: sinks in the stalls, big deal" (144).

By coupling dissimilar, incongruous entities, such similes express strangeness: in the characters themselves, in the world as they experience it, and in their lives. Odd, disparate things are fleetingly linked by the same synaptic leaps that also produce the wordplay in Moore's work. Her characters make quirky, un-likely associations that reveal concrete things (a face, a man) and abstract entities (life or love) in new lights. At the same time, however, these similes and metaphors are frequently reductive: a face that is likened to a cupcake is diminished in dignity (how-ever affectionate the thought), and love seems less profound and ponderous when associated with a lavatory stall. Such images are funny, but there is also pathos in them, speaking as they do of disappointment, disenchantment, and sometimes despair. As the title of the volume and the final story implies, these tales con-cern existences that are incomplete, deficient, unfulfilled—lives that are *like* life but not fully lives.

Midwest Stories

"Joy"

The midwestern setting of some of the stories encapsulates this idea of mediocrity, banality, or settling for second best. The main

character in "Joy" returns to her unnamed midwestern hometown after living in Oregon with a "daredevil" German boyfriend whose motto was "You only live at once" (57) and who
eventually betrayed her. Taking undemanding sales positions in
stores with fatuous names—"The Stout Shoppe" and "Swedish
Isle"—Jane exists within the narrow compass of her rented
house and the shopping mall, consciously shrinking from experiences that may unsettle her "little" life (66). Pleasantness is her
most excitable state because she regards more violent emotions
as dangerous: "There were only small joys in life—the big ones
were too complicated to be joys when you got all through—and
once you realized that, it took a lot of the pressure off" (52).
Accordingly her decision "not to risk" auditioning for the Community Chorus is only partly in case she should fail and thus lose
the daily pleasure of singing around her house and in the car.
Another reason is that the rapture of singing in a choir—"That
huge sound flying out over an audience, like a migration of birds,
like a million balloons!" (60)—is too frightening. She would
rather sing along to the radio while washing the dishes or driv-
ing her cat to the vet's.

If Jane's existence is bland and sometimes ridiculous—one of
her duties at the cheese shop is to hand out samples labeled
"HELLO MY NAME IS Swiss Almond Whip" (66)—it is nevertheless comfortingly "ordinary" (57). Her cat, Fluffers, is a less
volatile object of her affection than the unfaithful boyfriend
in Oregon, source of a sexual jealousy so intense that it transformed her from a mild midwesterner to "a wild West woman,
bursting into saloons" (52) to catch him drinking with other
women. Like female characters throughout Moore's fiction, Jane
experienced sexual love as a threat, not only to her psychological
equilibrium but also to her very sense of identity: "She was no
longer herself. She had become someone else" (52). By avoiding

sex, along with other exhilarating but dangerous pursuits such as waterskiing or surfing, she recovers and protects her stability.

Intermingled with the largely comic descriptions of this anodyne existence, however, are darker allusions to disease, decay, and death that reflect Jane's persistent morbid anxieties. At the "barest hint" (49) of fleas in Fluffers, she takes him to the vet for treatment, seized with irrational fears of contagion. There she is exposed to death when a much-loved cat called Gooby is admitted for thyroid surgery and returned to his owner lifeless. This episode is recounted with black humor (the cat is brought out in a cardboard box marked "DOLE PINEAPPLE," 63) but mortality is also the subject of a much stranger, antinaturalistic opening paragraph:

> It was a fall, Jane knew, when little things were being taken away. Fish washed ashore, and no one ate a clam to save their lives. Oystermen netted in the ocean beds, and the oysters were brought up dead. Black as rot and no one knew why. People far from either coast shuddered to think, saw the seas and then the whole planet rise in an angry, inky wave of chowder the size of a bowl. (49)

While this passage appears to locate uncanny phenomena on the seaboards, at a safe distance from inland populations, the second part of the paragraph describes the extension of the drought to the Midwest, recounting the bizarre hallucinations and deaths of thirst-maddened animals in futuristic terms that jar with the comic realism of most of the story.

"The Jewish Hunter"

The uneasy intermingling of humdrum daily life with intimations of mortality also characterizes "The Jewish Hunter," another story set in the midwestern "boonies" (117). The colorless small-town atmosphere of this location is adroitly evoked in details such as the "flavorless bladders of pasta" (118) served in the single Italian restaurant, but in this case it is portrayed as a culture that is alien to the main character, not comfortingly familiar as in "Joy." The focalizing character in "The Jewish Hunter" is a New York poet called Odette who takes intermittent library fellowships in the Midwest for the money. Her foreignness is signaled linguistically—the local vernacular is a "chirpy singsong" (120) that she cannot master—and in her tastes for good coffee, whiskey, cigarettes, and black clothing. Predisposed to regard the locals as "hillbilly . . . moron[s]" (118), she is jolted into a more complex view by the lawyer with whom she has an affair. A Jew in a locality where Jews are rare; "a kisser" (124) in a place where people "never kissed" (117), he repeatedly unsettles her preconceptions about both the Midwest and himself. By taking her to a local tourist attraction, the Cave of Many Mounds, he reveals unnerving depths of the landscape and its submarine ancient history: "The life and the sea of it trapped and never seeing light, a small moist cavern a million years in the making" (124).

The sexual suggestions in this passage are clear: what is "slowly opening, opening, and opening inside" (124) is not merely the Cave of Many Mounds (itself a sexually suggestive name) but Odette's submerged receptiveness to love. Following their trip underground, Odette and Pinky have sex, and their act of love is the "kindest" Odette has ever known. But the repeated word "opening" also implies exposure and vulnerability: Odette is falling in love with a man she hardly knows—an intimate who cradles her in bed and whispers her to sleep, and yet a stranger.

His strangeness is epitomized in two practices that she finds repugnant: watching Holocaust survival videos after having sex and going hunting. Her reaction to the first is to wonder "*who on earth*" he is and why she went to bed with him, especially given that all he can find to say in response to the images of Auschwitz and Treblinka in his videos is "heavy stuff" (125). "*Who on earth was entitled to such words?*" she wonders, and the reiterated phrase "on earth" evokes both the story's interest in the physical geography or geology of the Midwest and—through opposition—the idea of what is *not* on earth: an extraterrestrial other world of alien life forms that provides another metaphor for the perceived strangeness of Pinky. Only later, when Odette learns that Pinky's parents were killed in Nazi concentration camps, does her question seem, tacitly, to receive an answer: he is himself a Holocaust survivor and is therefore entitled to express himself on the subject in terms of his own choosing, even if she finds them inane.

Paradoxically, the discovery that Pinky is of European descent, with a personal connection to events far more momentous than any associated with the obscure provincial state in which he now lives, does not make it easier for Odette to love him. His sufferings evoke pity and tenderness—because he is an orphan, because he carries a scar on his face from an anti-Semitic assault in childhood, because he was consigned to a remedial school unit known as "The House" (136)—but this very tendency to absorb his pain increases her exposure to harm. The hunting episode encapsulates this sense of him as a threat to her safety. On the one hand Odette identifies Pinky with a man in the Holocaust video who, as a boy, was forced to sing for the Nazis (a boy with a voice "*beautiful like a bird*," 137). On the other he is a hunter, a killer of birds and other creatures, and she identifies herself with the deer that he first wounds, then kills, when they go hunting. The sex of the deer is not specified, but the language used to describe its wounded flight and eventual death has feminine connotations, not least in the reference to the "crimson gash" of its bleeding hip (132). As a Jew orphaned by the Nazis, Pinky is a victim of violence. In hunter's guise he is a perpetrator—a predatory male seduced by the machismo of guns and inflamed with a bloodlust that is indistinguishable from sexual desire. Odette's flight from the woods is an expression of moral disgust with blood sports, but it is also a retreat from the emotional complications that a relationship with Pinky entails. He embodies too many contradictions and complexities, produces too many conflicting reactions on her part, and she eventually runs away, back to the impersonal, ironic daily drama of life in New York.

"Two Boys"

If Odette is to some extent aligned with Pinky's hunting kill, a female protagonist is again associated with dead animals and meat in "Two Boys." In this case the connection, both figurative and circumstantial, is butchery: Mary lives above the Alexander Hamilton Meat Company in Cleveland, Ohio, and is daily confronted with a river of blood in the gutter and "pale, fatty carcasses, hooked and naked" (4). The material and metaphorical attributes of this enforced contact are intermingled: the "refrigerated smell" (4) that follows her upstairs and into her apartment is both the actual stench of raw meat and a reminder of mortality, a spiritual taint.

Sexual symbolism is prominent in the passages concerning the meat company; as in "Joy" and "The Jewish Hunter" there is a powerful association between sex and death. Both female and male bodies are evoked in these descriptions. The displayed carcases conjure images of women as merchandise, but strings of "phallic" sausages (18) also portray men as faceless sexual entities, reduced to metonymical members. It is sex itself—meaty, visceral, palpable—that Mary sees represented in the butcher's goods, which explains why the smell of meat induces in her a "vague shame" (4).

A sensitive person in the early stages of a nervous breakdown and involved simultaneously with two men, Mary is both oversexed and guilt-ridden on the subject of sex. Her sense of herself as greedy and base is fed by a friend's reaction to her two-timing: "*You hog*" (8)—an image that also identifies Mary with the pig carcases on the Hamilton Pork Company premises. Afflicted with a doubly negative self-image—as pig and pork, the emblems of unconstrained appetite and resistless object of consumption—she compensates by dressing in white and reading Bible poetry in the local park, trying to remain "unsullied" by grass stains, dog mess, or undue proximity to couples "making out" (3). Returning home from these supposedly purifying afternoons unavoidably, however, involves reentering the world of sexed identities through the male-dominated butchery business: "men unloading meat in front of her building" (3–4), men wearing "red-stained doctors' coats" (4)—masquerading as healers although they deal in death. The way the story cuts between Mary's passing encounters with these "meat men" (7) and her interactions with the other men in her life, her two unsatisfactory boyfriends, implies that Mary regards her lovers as potential butchers who may prove capable, figuratively, of making her bleed and carving her up.

Although "Two Boys" is set in Cleveland, Moore has admitted that in truth it is "clearly a New York story." "I think I just decided I had too many stories that were set in New York—

I wanted to get out of that city."[8] In light of this comment it is unsurprising that "Two Boys" shows much less regional character than other midwestern stories in *Like Life* or elsewhere. Unlike "Joy" and "The Jewish Hunter," it contains almost no Midwest comedy. There are no humorous scenes in parochial shopping malls or backwoods bars, no jokes about "*Horses' douvers*" (58) or "*po biz*" (118). Short sections set variously in Mary's apartment, the park, and Boy Number One's office together create comparatively little sense of place; only Ottawa, where she takes a two-week vacation, is systematically described. The absence of concrete contextualizing details increases the impression that the setting of this story is Mary's inner world, inside her mind. "*My life is very strange,*" she says at one point, and it is this strangeness that the tale foregrounds. As her nervous breakdown progresses she takes to staying in her apartment, spending long periods in an uncertain state between dream and waking, occasionally speaking on the telephone but more often allowing the answering machine to pick up. The messages she receives are frequently interrogative: Boy Number One, who does not love her, saying, "I've forgotten when you were coming home. Is it today?" (15) and Boy Number Two, who loves her too much, pleading, "I know you're there. Will you please pick up the phone?" (16). The disembodied voices acquire a hallucinatory quality, particularly when the messages are reiterated, as when "a strange girl" repeatedly calls and asks, "Who are you? What is your name?" (15). Voicing Mary's own sense of uncertain identity, the girl invites interpretation as imaginary, a projection of Mary's subconscious, and thus joins a line of ambiguously phantasmal female figures in Moore's fiction: "strange girls," not least in the sense of being strange to, or estranged from, themselves.

To this category, and again seeming to give material form to Mary's mental disintegration, belong two females whom Mary encounters in the park: a twenty year old "swirling about" to tape-recorded music and representing, in Mary's eyes, the consequences of being "dreamy and unpopular in high school" (17) and an aggressive eleven year old who accosts her on four occasions and eventually follows her home. Mary sees the dancing woman as a cautionary spectacle, a warning of what she may become if she loses what little remains of her dignity and sanity. The terms in which the eleven year old is portrayed are more complex. She behaves in a hardened, tough manner, spitting and sneering; she wears lipstick and a halterneck top, refers constantly to her "boyfriends," and possesses sexually precocious knowledge in her "bulleted heart" (19) but is twice associated with the frail beauty of a bird through images focusing on the delicate bones in her back. Mary fears her because her mocking gaze seems penetrating and knowing, appearing to fathom the secret of Mary's sexual infidelity; but at the same time the girl can be seen as a manifestation of degenerate sexuality—a debauched child who makes lewd comparisons between her ex-boyfriends' penises and a string of sausages, a prematurely sexual "little girl" (17) who embodies Mary's sexual neuroses and guilty conscience.

New York Tales

Preoccupations with death, sex, and psychology—the disturbing life of the mind—emerge in the five New York stories even more powerfully than in the three that are set in the Midwest. Associated for much of the twentieth century with modernist dehumanisation and alienation,[9] New York was also, in the late 1980s, when Moore was writing these stories, widely perceived as threatening and dangerous—a setting ideally adapted to stories about fear. At about the same time, Susan Minot was using a metropolitan setting to portray disequilibrium or breakdown in stories such as "City Night" and "Sparks."[10] Moore employs a similar technique, investing her depictions of New York with strongly psychological implications.

"Places to Look for Your Mind"

References to women losing their minds pervade Moore's work, starting, as chapter 2 showed, in *Self-Help*. Many of her heroines, through loss or lack of romantic love, illness, childlessness, loneliness, or a general feeling of not belonging in their social or cultural world, are in mental conditions bordering on insanity. The metaphor of losing one's mind is characteristic of Moore in that it reifies the mind, portraying it as a contingent property of personhood—something that can be possessed or mislaid. The title "Places to Look for Your Mind" presupposes a lost mind, and there are various hints that the mind in question is that of the well-meaning but unappreciated Millie Keegan, a middle-aged housewife whose life is defined by what is missing from it: her son, who severed ties with the family ten years previously; her cold and ungrateful daughter, temporarily abroad; and an occupation, since the recycling business she tried to start never really got off the ground. The text is punctuated by allusions to her absent mind: her spoonerism about being ever needful of the minds of others (99); an analogy between her mind and an unwanted garbage barge that is in the news, wandering from port to port with "nowhere to go" (103); her husband Hane's "old joke" about looking for your mind in the refrigerator (98).

Hane, a college teacher, also refers to the mindlessness of "kids" (103), and it is the mental health of the Keegans' young male visitor from England that turns out to be most precarious.

Traveling from England to America, commuting from New Jersey to Manhattan, departing suddenly for California but just as suddenly returning home, John Spee is the most conspicuous wanderer in the story, repeatedly making journeys by plane, train, and greyhound bus. Since the title associates "places" with the search for one's mind, John's roving from place to place reads as a quest for a mental equilibrium he has lost. New Jersey, Los Angeles, and especially Manhattan prove inimical to his search, presenting him, not with a restored self-image as a sane and happy person, but with ubiquitous incarnations of madness.

The story opens with a banner welcoming John to America and goes on to mention America several times, underlining its own status as a study of the national culture and psyche, both of which are found lacking. Having discovered John's lists of "Crazy People" encountered in Manhattan (a man in a business suit, screaming; a woman in a park, shrieking at her dog; a woman in a coffee shop shouting at her fork), Millie understands his disillusionment with the city and by extension the whole continent: "How disappointing America must seem. To wander the streets of a city that was not yours, a city with its back turned, to be a boy from far away and step ashore here, one's imagination suddenly so concrete and mistaken, how could that not break your heart?" (112).

"You're Ugly, Too" and "Starving Again"

Millie's insight summarizes the inflated status of New York in the Western imagination and the false expectations that this produces. The idea of the city tends to exceed the reality. In "concrete" rather than imagined form it is hostile and unknowable, an alien and alienating environment. The protagonist of the well-known story "You're Ugly, Too" experiences it in this way, and Moore uses the plot device of a Halloween party to dramatize the city's strangeness. Originally from the East Coast state of Maryland and now a college teacher in Illinois, Zoë Hendricks, a brunette, is taken for Spanish by the uniformly blonde midwesterners. But when she travels to New York to visit her sister, she feels equally set apart from New Yorkers. These perceptions of distance and difference are reflected in references, throughout the story, to nonhuman life forms. Zoë's earrings "jut . . . out from the side of her head like antennae" (68), and there are metaphors featuring a blue jay, an ant, a dog, a "wrongheaded" bird (78), fish, "toad-faced cicadas" (79), apes, gorillas, worms, bugs, and bowerbirds. It is the fancy dress party, however, that gives most concrete form to Zoë's sense of New York and its inhabitants as alien or inhuman, with guests attending in costumes drawn from the animal world (an ape, a tropical fish), mythology (a leprechaun, some witches), and processed food (a frozen dinner).

Zoë, staying closer than most to the Halloween theme, goes as a "bonehead" (71)—one of the stock characters in horror films but also slang for a crazed or demented person. Her mental instability, which mounts rapidly during the limited time frame of the story, is strongly associated with her sexed identity, not only because she feels unattractive to men but also, and more seriously, because her body has betrayed her by developing suspected cancer in the very region (vaguely identified as her abdomen) where she would like to conceive a child. Zoë's sexual dysphoria is embodied in the naked-woman costume worn by a man named Earl with whom her sister tries to fix her up at the party. Consisting of a body stocking sporting steel-wool pubic hair and "large rubber breasts" (82), this outfit is a parody of female sexuality, which, though synthetic rather than literally carnal, nevertheless has some points in common with the butcher's-meat symbols of corporeal sexuality in "Two Boys," since the breasts are described as "protruding like hams" (82). In a sense Earl in woman's guise can be seen as Zoë's alter ego —another of the figures Moore introduces to reflect, project, or mock female characters' insecurity. As the party proceeds his fake female body dramatizes the dysfunctioning of Zoë's gendered anatomy as well as her mental disintegration: the pubic and axillary hair slips out of position and one of the rubber breasts becomes unmoored, shifting round until it is tucked under his arm "like a baguette" (87).

"You're Ugly, Too" ends with Zoë giving Earl a shove from behind that nearly pushes him over the rail of the balcony on which they have been standing to talk. Despite Zoë's inadequate assurances that she was "just kidding" (91), this recklessly aggressive gesture is less comical than disturbing—an enactment of Zoë's unbalanced inner state and her own danger of going, metaphorically if not literally, over the edge. If it is intended as a practical joke, it is as dark and tasteless as much of the verbal humor—and many of the sight gags—throughout Moore's fiction: more "terrible" than "funny," to slightly misquote Zoë's response to another tasteless joke. Robert Chodat categorizes the stunt on the balcony among Zoë's "crazed fantasies," which far from being frivolous, reflect her "existential terror" and fear of "decay and death."[11] A related way of looking at it is as a displaced suicide fantasy, like Mary's daydream about jumping through an office-block window in "Two Boys": "Mary was staring past him out the window. There were women who leaped through such glass. Just got a running start and did it" (11).

One function of the balcony episode in "You're Ugly, Too," then, is as the climax of psychological implications that build up throughout the story. Like most of the pieces in *Like Life*, this is a story that operates at various levels, the least complicated of which is as a narrative concerning a journey and a party. At this level there are rational explanations for Zoë's perceptions of strangeness in the world and the people around her: she is in an unfamiliar city and is socializing with people dressed in bizarre costumes. At another level references to Zoë's general unhappiness, loneliness, and doubtful health suggest that the strangeness of Manhattan and its residents is more subjective than objective: her unstable state of mind distorts her perceptions. Read in this way, details such as the party guests' fancy dress have metaphorical as well as literal significance in the text; they are properties of the storyline but also emblems of Zoë's encroaching madness. In this reading Moore's aims go beyond straightforward storytelling into a realm where the main value of certain plot elements is figurative, and it is this kind of aesthetic that seems to be in operation in the balcony episode. If the events of the story up to this point balance literal status with metaphorical meaning, Zoë's attempt to push Earl off the balcony shifts that balance, carrying more weight as a symbolic than as a literal action. Its excessive nature makes it implausible or unrealistic, a violation of the norms of social intercourse so shocking that it implies authorial disregard for plausibility or mimetic illusion. Moore seems not, here, to be aiming for literary realism or verisimilitude but trying to capture the quality of Zoë's subjective experience—how it feels to be Zoë—by less naturalistic means. The improbability of Zoë's attempting to kill Earl does not matter; what matters is the incident's expressive potential, its power of conveying Zoë's unbalanced mental condition.

To put it another way, the function of the balcony scene in "You're Ugly, Too" and of strange episodes or images in other stories is not to be mimetically lifelike, adhering to "the norms of realist fiction,"[12] but to help represent what a particular life feels like, whether that life be Zoë's, Mary's, Millie's, Jane's, Odette's, or indeed Pinky's or John Spee's. The invitation to play with the words "like" and "life," to view them in different combinations and consider the various permutations in their meanings, is present in the title of the collection, signaling a reflexive interest in how fiction operates and how literature relates to life. Moore never writes in a wholly conventional realist vein. In *Like Life*, even the naturalistic short piece "Starving Again" ends with a startling moment in which Dennis makes a physical grab at Mave across the restaurant table and harries her in a "high and watery" voice (148), causing a disturbance that, within the storyworld, dramatizes his inebriation and sexual need but that in its unexpected violence also, at a stylistic level, dramatizes the momentary disruption of the predominantly realist framework.

"Vissi d'Arte" and "Like Life"

Two stories that conspicuously explore questions of what is real—in relation to phenomena within the world of the fiction and with regard to issues of literary realism—are "Vissi d'Arte" and "Like Life." Both, appropriately enough, feature main characters who are involved in the arts, and both employ conspicuous alienation techniques to represent these characters' deficient, defective lives in New York. The protagonist of "Vissi d'Arte" —a phrase taken from Puccini's opera *Tosca* and meaning "I've lived for art"—is the impoverished playwright Harry DeLeo, whose devotion to a pure but unsuccessful ideal of literary production entails the sacrifice of material comfort, social standing, and sexual love. His girlfriend leaves him in favor of "a *real* life" (23), voicing a feeling that Harry's existence is too makeshift, disorganized, and eccentric—too unlike other people's lives—

to count as real. As the narrative progresses, Harry becomes increasingly disengaged from the mainstream of society. He develops a preference for remote and disembodied interactions, such as telephone conversations, over face-to-face contact, and when he is driven out of his squalid apartment by the noisy idling engines and noxious fumes of huge trucks parked outside his building overnight, he joins the nocturnal street life of criminals, drug addicts, and the homeless.

Increasingly psychological connotations accrue around questions of what is "real" at the same time as the story itself becomes less conventionally realistic. Harry's nighttime disturbances by monstrous trucks have the estranged quality of a bad dream both in his mind and on the page; the narrative mode matches his mental state and is lifelike in the sense of conveying the texture of his subjective experience. Similarly the exaggerated episodes featuring defective plumbing in Harry's bathroom, as rats wash up in the toilet bowl and the bath taps disgorge a repulsive likeness of "miso soup with scallions" (32), capture Harry's sense of being, like a character in a play he is planning, "shackled in nightmare, and in that constant state of daydream that nightmare gives conception to" (42). Although vermin and bad plumbing are objective facts of New York life, Moore's use of them goes beyond naturalism; they become tropes for Harry's inner condition.

Equally, the vicious punishment beating of a shoplifter that Harry witnesses in a grocery store, while a plausible reflection of New York's violent culture, is so brutal as to seem, again, nightmarish. With clear echoes of the butchery in "Two Boys," the shoplifter is beaten like meat in the back room until he can "no longer call out," then dragged like a carcass through the shop, his blood smearing the floor. The shoplifter's substantial, corporeal "reality" is insisted on in the description of this incident, but the police dismiss Harry's report in terms that deny its reality, ambiguously downplaying its seriousness and/or implying that he imagined it: "We got real things" (41). The word "real" in this response has a double meaning within the bounds of the story—serious rather than trivial, actual as opposed to imaginary—to which can be added a third, metafictional construction relating to the uncertain status of the incident as a faithful representation of Manhattan life or a symbolic vignette intended to dramatize Harry's nervous breakdown.

This story's reflexive interest in literary or other mediated representations of life emerges in several ways. Harry's one-off theatrical success, *For Hours See a Ranger,* dramatizes the marginalized observer role he occupies in relation to the vibrant swim of Manhattan life in that it features a character, the eponymous ranger, whose role is to stand stage left for the duration of the play, watching the action unfold. Later the unscrupulous television producer Glen Scarp, for whom Harry considers writing material, fictionalizes Harry's life by using anecdotes about DeLeo family history as the basis for storylines in his show, shamelessly transforming real people—Harry's relations—into a "fascinating bunch of characters!" (36). The dramatic arts, visual mediation, and ideas of virtual reality recur at the end of the story, in connection with another kind of spectacle and a different type of screen: a sex show that Harry visits out of desperate loneliness and the smeared glass partition that divides customers from dancers. If all of the stories in this collection to some extent concern unfilled needs and hungers, Harry's pitiful act of pressing his mouth to the screened-off breast of a sex worker is one of the most graphic and moving dramatizations of sexual and emotional starvation. The screen reifies the divide between the human intimacy Harry yearns for and the simulation of this, which is all that the peep show trades in, and the story ends with a meditation on feigned love and the sorrow of resorting to a commercial performance that is only "like something real" (48).

Mediation of "real" human experience—for instance, in the Holocaust survival videos in "The Jewish Hunter"—is one of the structuring themes of *Like Life*, culminating in the radically defamiliarizing title story. This narrative's position at the end of the book reflects its status as the most "unrealistic" story in the collection as well as the way it draws together various threads that run through all the preceding stories: illness; decay and pollution; fear and danger; the failure of love. "Like Life" is written in science fiction style that builds on passing references to outer space throughout the volume, from the "message from outer space" delivered to Mary as a ball of spittle (6) to Pinky's view of Odette as "cute but from outer space" (122). This story presents a futuristic scenario of a politically totalitarian New York where television is compulsory—officially for the dissemination of government information but allegedly also for surveillance. Films about "people with plates in their heads" (149) suggest extraterrestrial invasion and possession; while the heroine, Mamie, worries that objects "implanted" in her ("fillings, earrings, contraceptives," 150) may be devices intended to turn her into a "ventriloquized" (151) dummy for the government.

Moore's "pilfering" of science fiction and political allegory here anticipates a comment she makes in a review of Margaret Atwood's futuristic novel *Oryx and Crake*, where she describes literary dystopia as "a bad dream of our present time."[13] In Moore's case this purpose is signaled in the title of the story, which invites consideration of how far Mamie's existence in a diseased and dangerous dictatorship is "like life" in America in the early 1990s. But the collocation of "like" with "life" has several other bearings on the story. For one thing it suggests that Mamie's life is not a fully realized autonomous experience but one she is "forced to live out," as she puts it herself, "in imitation" (151). Like Breckie in "Vissi d'Arte," Mamie complains of the impoverished, improvised life she leads with her struggling-artist boyfriend. Mamie and Rudy live in South Brooklyn, in a converted beauty parlor, not a "real" house (153), and Mamie dreams of a beautiful, old-fashioned, empty house with "a cupola, gables, and a porch" (149). Having decided to leave Rudy and actively hunting for a place of her own, she discovers a dilapidated Edwardian Gothic house with all these features plus a garden. However, this house, representing the antithesis of the futuristic urban landscape she inhabits and seeming to offer the promise of "another existence" (157), is inaccessible: the iron gate is locked.

Dwelling places also feature in an apocalyptic dream in which Mamie discovers underneath her apartment a whole house inhabited by birds and belonging to her, and identifies this as "the end of the world" (174). This morbid vision fits in with another connotation of "like" and "life": the story's extended meditation on death. Although death is the antithesis of life, in one sense the *least* lifelike experience, it is life's inevitable counterpart, its verbal and metaphysical alter ego. In this story it is omnipresent—in the toxic tap water, the streets infested with the destitute dying, the Gowanus Canal murders of women, Rudy's increasingly violent artworks, and even the children's history book that Mamie is illustrating, which concerns the spread of disease from European settlers to native Americans. At a personal level for Mamie, the specter of death overshadows her life in the form of what her doctor identifies as precancerous growths in her throat and on her back. An exchange between Mamie and the doctor underlines the immanence of death in life. Confused by a diagnosis that seems to place her in a condition *prior* to illness, she asks, "*Pre*cancer? . . . Isn't that . . . like *life*?" (152).

In spite of this morbidity "Like Life" does not end in unmitigated darkness. One of the many ailing entities in the story has been the love between Mamie and Rudy, which has "begun to sicken" (159), but there is a qualified note of optimism when Mamie is relieved to discover that Rudy is not, as she had suspected, the Gowanus murderer and is alive rather than having committed suicide. The subsequent rapprochement between them, although not an idealized romantic reunion, suggests that Mamie has accepted a pragmatic philosophy, which she tried to articulate earlier in the story. It is not necessary, she points out to Rudy, to feel passionate about life: "'You don't have to love it'" (173). There is a lesser option that people can settle for, but she cannot find the word to identify it: "'You only have to—' She couldn't think of what" (173). The missing verb, love's diminished counterpart, is "like," as another character in the story, a secretary at a Manhattan publishing company, could easily tell her. "'I don't have a love life,'" this woman explains to Mamie, "'I have a *like* life'" (173), thus advocating, like Jane in "Joy," moderate emotion over intense passion and its attendant pains.

Conclusion

A recurring motif in Moore's work is the idea of the narrated and dramatized life. Her characters conceptualize and comment on their lives as texts or enactments: case studies in self-help literature, roles in plays, narratives in films, books, and television programs. This conceit mirrors and magnifies characters' subjective feelings of detachment from their experiences and relationships, and their estrangement from the overmediated society in which they live. "Like Life" takes the conceit to the extreme, presenting a dystopia that combines the hyperreal technology and mediation of late consumer capitalism with all *too* real material squalor, decay, and violence. Like a science fiction movie that Odette watches with Pinky in "The Jewish Hunter," this story is "an elaborate urban allegory, full of disease and despair" (119).

The emotions that Moore's characters experience in the nightmarish world of "Like Life" are the same ones they suffer in other stories—above all, disappointment, loneliness, and various forms of heartfelt "terror"[14]—and its fantastic dimensions represent a deliberate aesthetic strategy for convincing fictional treatment of these feelings. The futuristic form is an extension of the defamiliarization technique Moore uses to a greater or lesser extent throughout *Like Life,* an approach that draws attention to the fictiveness of stories without negating their power of representing how human experience feels and in that sense being "lifelike; absolutely lifelike."[15]

Here as elsewhere a full appreciation of Moore's fiction requires enjoyment of her self-conscious, and sometimes playful or daring, artfulness. Her quirkiest characters and most far-fetched events knowingly transgress the boundaries of realistic literature, and even the more naturalistic stories revolving around "ordinary" people in recognizable situations acquire an odd, improbable, distanced quality from the idiosyncratic focus and the comic, ironizing tone of the narration. All art is imitation or re-creation and therefore in a narrow sense "unreal," but readers of *Like Life* and other of Moore's works repeatedly attest to her gift for capturing the mood of "real lives" and "'represent[ing]' a contemporary world that . . . feels refreshingly *real.*"[16]

CHAPTER 5

Who Will Run the Frog Hospital?

The early 1990s, following publication of *Like Life*, saw growing acknowledgment of Moore's talent in forms ranging from prestigious fellowships to literary prizes.[1] Her public profile was raised by the appearance in the *New Yorker,* at regular intervals during 1990–93, of stories that would return between the covers of *Birds of America* at the end of the decade and by pieces in the *New York Times,* including major book reviews and political commentaries. These were turbulent times in the foreign and domestic arenas, with the demise of the Soviet Union as the United States' only rival superpower and the fallout of years of relatively unconstrained capitalism on both sides of the Atlantic. In an op-ed column in November 1992, some nine months after the end of the first Gulf War and on the day Bill Clinton surged past Ross Perot at the ballot box to oust George Bush from the White House, Moore made clear her disenchantment with the entire American political scene.[2] Satirically characterizing all three presidential hopefuls as equally undesirable suitors in a long and dreary courtship of "*the American people,*" she poked fun at their respective "courting styles" as equally empty performances, a matter of mere "attitudes and tricks" revolving around "televised flattery, . . . bad candy, [and] shifting hair styles."

Moore's repetition in this column of the phrase "*the American people*"—six times and always ironically italicized—conveys distrust of the candidates' repeated appeals to national identity.

It suggests that "*the American people*" was in her eyes a slippery fiction, part and parcel of a presidential campaign that was conducted "through the looking glass. In some other . . . Lewis Carroll world" where words meant whatever Clinton, Bush, and Perot wanted them to. "Voters in Wonderland" is interesting not only as a statement of Moore's political skepticism at the end of the first Bush administration but also for the way it associates fictions of nation with storybook fantasy. Wonderland here is a metaphor for an America conjured up by politicians, a fabulous world whose inhabitants are far more susceptible to seduction than the actual American voters on "the real side" of the mirror.

Theme Park America

A similar metaphor for America-as-fiction—in this case Storyland rather than Wonderland—is central to the book Moore must have been working on at the time her *New York Times* column was published: her second novel, *Who Will Run the Frog Hospital?*[3] Possibly based on a New Hampshire theme park of the same name founded by Bob and Ruth Morrell in 1954, Moore's Storyland is owned by a superficially idealistic businessman whose credo is nationalism: "I believe in America" (112). Its theme song invokes the revered American ideal of family life —ironized in Moore's rendering by respelling, hyphenation, and an exclamation mark: "*Bring the whole famil-lee!*"—and promises wish fulfillment, albeit on a humorously selective basis ("*a place where a lot / of your dreams come true*") (9). The implied happy ending does not materialize for all visitors, however. Despite the song's assurances that Storyland is "not a sad or gory land" (9), in one family's experience it is both gory and sad, when a roller-coaster car derails and a boy loses his legs. The name of the ride in question—The Lost Mine—invites gruesome reinterpretation in light of this loss, if "mine" is construed as a possessive pronoun applying to the child's limbs. After the accident the blood is hosed away, employees dressed as cowboys disperse the crowd, and by means of a pay-off and a cover-up, the owner manages to keep the incident quiet, until in time its origins in fact or fiction are obscured: it becomes a "persistent rumour," then "a less persistent rumour," and eventually "a story, as if from long ago" (89).

A story culminating in dismemberment is not typical of the narratives enacted at Storyland. Although the books and nursery rhymes that "*come to life*" (9) there—Cinderella, Little Bo Peep, Snow White—may contain grotesque incidents, they generally have happy, even sentimental, endings. The amusements at Storyland borrow from these stock narratives at random, jumbling together fictional characters and episodes with no coherent rationale, so that Storyland as a whole is meaningless, devoid of plot or structure. Insofar as there is an overall design, it is venal: the gift shop is positioned near the exit as a final opportunity to extract money from visitors. As a metaphor for America that is founded on simulation and characterized by lack of meaning, the park recalls Jean Baudrillard's pronouncement: "It is Disneyland that is authentic here!"[4] In his view simulation was so widespread in late-twentieth-century American culture that an openly imitative and derivative environment such as a theme park—an environment explicitly organized around inauthenticity—possessed a paradoxical authenticity. The most real America was artificial, a reproduction, and in order to understand the nation one had to "enter the fiction of America, enter America as fiction."[5]

The model of America that Moore presents in *Who Will Run the Frog Hospital?* resembles Baudrillard's caricature in several respects. The vicinity of Horsehearts, New York, where much of the action takes place, contains several sites that simulate and capitalize on incidents in American history: Lafayette Café, General Montcalm Inn, and Fond du Lac Fort, "reconstructed for the tourists" (42) with fake cannons and teenagers doing summer jobs impersonating British soldiers. These sites draw on and reenact narratives of American nation building out of the same mixture of nostalgia, national sentiment, and commercial calculation that motivates the reconstruction of fairytales at Storyland. Dickie Ress, proprietor of an attraction unashamedly named "Fort Ress," is in the same mold as Storyland proprietor Frank Morenton. Both embody traits that Baudrillard identifies as typically American: lack of irony and sophistication, undiscriminating enthusiasm, and an absence of principles—qualities, incidentally, that are also evident in Moore's satirical pen portraits of Clinton, Bush, and Perot in "Voters in Wonderland." These are, on the one hand, earnest, credulous, and ingenuous patriots employing the affable idiom of the common man. "Heck," Moore in the *New York Times* imagines Perot thinking on a talk-show stage, "look what he was doing: he was running for President!" Morenton speaks in the same down-home register. "Let's just call it even Steven," he says in relation to an employee's thefts from Storyland. But he is motivated, like a politician, by a desire to protect his public image from "scandal and commotion" (112). His constituents are the American families whose interests he prides himself on serving, but there is self-interest, too, behind his philosophy of service. In the final analysis those American families pay for his shiny white convertible, and he is as intent on keeping them happy as are Clinton, Bush, and Perot (or Moore's re-creations of them) on sweet talking "*the American people.*"

Memory Lane

Through the extended metaphor of Storyland, then, Moore represents America as a theme park in dodgy hands. This is not the only figurative function of Morenton's empire, however; it also serves as a metaphor for Moore's novel itself, a novel that one reviewer summed up as a "sad, witty, disillusioned fairy tale."[6] In its dramatization of fictions associated with childhood, Storyland alludes metafictionally to the way in which the novel as a whole is constructed—around episodes drawn from the early lives of Berie Carr and Silsby Chaussée. As teenagers Berie and Sils work at Storyland as costumed employees and hang out during their lunch breaks in a section of the theme park called Memory Lane. As an adult Berie travels down her personal memory lane to construct a retrospective narrative of their friendship. Berie and Sils, not Hansel and Gretel or the Old Woman Who Lived in a Shoe, are the "storybook characters" around whom that fictional world (or story land) revolves.

An interest in the operation of memory is apparent from the opening paragraph of *Who Will Run the Frog Hospital?* in which the middle-aged Berie, visiting Paris with her husband, states that she is eating brains "for a flashback" (3). By consuming an unknown animal's "*cervelles*," she hopes to stimulate recollective processes in her own brain—"something Proustian," as she puts it: "All that forgotten childhood" (3). In a similar phrase nearly ten years later, Moore would refer to John Updike's "Proustian retrievals of childhood" in some of his early stories.[7] Berie's Proustian retrievals in *Frog Hospital* together make up (an apt phrase) the story of her Horsehearts years. This story is longer than the present-tense framing narrative set in Paris and, to judge by the critical literature, is the focus of most readers' interest. But in the first published version of material from *Who Will Run the Frog Hospital?* there is no flashback. The *New Yorker* story "Paris" covers a three-week period in the city of that name and broadly corresponds to the Parisian sections of *Frog Hospital*.[8] Some of Berie's unhappy personal history makes its way in, but its explicit references to the past are of a more public nature, revolving around French history in the mid–twentieth century.

"Paris" was not originally written as a free-standing story, according to Moore.

> My editor at the *New Yorker* at the time noticed that it might make a story, and when she pointed it out to me, I became interested in it as such. . . . I thought it made for a moody little American-in-Paris tale. So I published it separately as "Paris" in the *New Yorker* and thought of it as separate from the novel, and was interested in it as something thing completely distinct from it, something created *from* it.[9]

Reading "Paris" alongside *Who Will Run the Frog Hospital?* throws light on the themes, including history and memory, that the shorter text introduces and the longer work develops. "Paris" is very much an expatriate narrative, portraying French history and culture from the perspective of a foreign national. The cityscape contains widespread reminders, in Berie's eyes, of the French capital's history of occupation by and collaboration with Nazi Germany in World War II. Posters for an Audrey Hepburn festival showing Hepburn in evening dress remind Berie of Anne Frank, and she imagines her Jewish husband Daniel summarizing the "essence of Paris" as "Anne Frank in an evening gown" ("Paris," 86)—the city's glamor being tainted, in other words, by its role in delivering Jews into the hands of the Nazis. Berie's uncomfortable consciousness of French collusion in the Holocaust is also evident in her perception of municipal flower-beds as "full of pansies whose triangular, black centers are like the mustache of Hitler himself" ("Paris," 90). Oppressive mistreatment of Algerian immigrants in the 1960s and ongoing racial discrimination are mentioned as more recent chapters in what Berie regards as French "abominable history" ("Paris," 90).

One of the most striking aspects of Berie's attitude to this "abominable history" is her pessimism regarding the moral utility of recording it for posterity:

> There is no place to put such facts, not properly. There is only one's own mournful horror, one's worthless moral vanity—which can do nothing. The bad news of the world, like most bad news, has no place to go. You tack it to the bulletin-board part of your heart. You say, *Look*. You say, *See*. That is all. ("Paris," 90)

Coming from a curator (Berie works for the American Historical Society) visiting a city with a pronounced "curatorial culture," this is a bleak assessment. It suggests that past events can be recorded but not remedied: memory is an impotent faculty. The passage reifies unwelcome "facts" and "bad news" as artifacts that can be exhibited but to no purpose. Displaying them is an end in itself, not a means to an ameliorated past or—by implication in the definitive statement "That is all"—a less horrifying future.

Although this meditation on Berie's part is concerned with a shameful chapter, as she sees it, in French political history, its central trope—of knowledge as an object on display—echoes an earlier passage concerning France's artistic heritage. After a brief visit to a much-changed Louvre, Berie reflects on the unproductive, self-perpetuating logic of memorialization: "My own memory, from a trip ten years ago, is a tired, old coin. Who will house that? Who will house the Museum of Museums, in order to show us how museums once were?" ("Paris," 86). Berie's nostalgia for the earlier design and layout of the Louvre is itself conceptualized, here, as an unwanted artifact. Like the disturbing facts of French anti-Semitism and racism, it has "no place to go." Berie's repeated question about housing that memory emphasizes the futile circularity of remembering: even if a home is found for it, it will remain a "tired, old coin," a worthless item of obsolete currency.

Emotional Exile

The mood of nostalgia in "Paris," and the sense of Berie as outcast or exiled, extend to the two personal relationships in which she is involved: her failing marriage and her friendship with a female contemporary from college. To start with her marriage, the problems between Berie and her husband Daniel are those that also afflict couples in *Self-Help, Anagrams,* and *Like Life:* childlessness and infidelity. Early on in the story Berie describes Daniel explaining to French strangers, in an English "patois" that mimics French, "*We, us, have no little ones*" ("Paris," 84). The reason is that both Berie and Daniel carry the gene for Tay Sachs disease, an illness that causes progressive destruction of the central nervous system and is relatively common among the French Canadian and Jewish populations to which they respectively belong. Biological parenting is consequently out of the question: in their house in America the upstairs room that might have become the baby's room is instead "the Maybe's Room," kept empty for a possible adopted child—a child, as Daniel quips sadly, acquired "retail rather than wholesale" ("Paris," 84). The prospect of adoption seems diminished, however, by the estrangement between Berie and Daniel caused partly by his affairs with other women and partly by an injury to her hip that he inflicted by pushing her downstairs during an argument about his womanizing. Repeated references to the aching joint imply that the damage, not only to her body but to their marriage, is permanent. Valiantly though they try to reconnect and make their "minds . . . one" ("Paris," 84), the tone of their repartee is frequently sorrowful, and Daniel fears that like his father he will end up leaving for another woman, with the implication that Berie will suffer the same fate as his mother, who "lost her mind" ("Paris," 91).

The parlous state of her marriage, and specifically the history of her limp, are subjects Berie would like to discuss honestly with her old college friend Marguerite. She imagines the course of their bilingual conversation—"*Can I tell you the truth? . . . Bien sûr. . . .* Daniel pushed me down the stairs" ("Paris," 87)—but is deterred by the prospect of Marguerite's disbelieving reaction:

> *Non, tu blagues!* she'd say.
> And I would continue. *Non, je ne blague pas!* (87)

The English meaning of Berie's final admission, "No, I'm not joking," goes to the heart of her predicament. Her husband no longer loves her; he has harmed her, and this is no laughing matter. Marguerite, by contrast with Berie, is beautiful, chic, and independent, an artist rather than a mere curator—and, most symbolically, a woman with "good legs" ("Paris," 87) instead of a bad hip. Berie's decision not to take Marguerite into her confidence about the disintegration of her marriage is reflected figuratively in a scene in which the two women sit outside together drinking beers and eating pastries known as "divorces." When Marguerite raises the topic of relations between the sexes, Berie's mouth is "full of Divorce" but she doesn't translate her feelings into speech.

Berie's inability to confide in Marguerite seems symptomatic of her adult lack of intimate companionship: no mention is made of close friends back home in America, and her reported conversations with neighbors there characterize her as feeling "empty" and "disconnected" ("Paris," 91). If, as she says, she has a "crush" on Marguerite, it is not nearly as intense and absorbing as the crush the adolescent Berie has on Silsby Chaussée in *Frog Hospital*, though there are similarities. Marguerite, like Sils, is "dazzling" ("Paris," 86), and Berie's role, as with Sils, is to admire and amuse her. They discuss clothes, mess around with makeup, drink beers, laugh immoderately, and talk about sex. But all this is in the context of a single day together, not, as in the case of Berie and Sils, the everyday familiarity of shared lives. Even as fellow students, Marguerite and Berie were "not that close" (87), and Marguerite's only concrete memento of that era, a copy of the "Desiderata" hanging on her wall, strikes Berie as misplaced.

Friendship and Sex

Nevertheless the episode in "Paris" featuring Marguerite provides one of the strongest links between the story and the novel. *Who Will Run the Frog Hospital?* is Moore's contribution to a literature of formative female friendship that also, in North America, includes works by Joyce Carol Oates, Margaret Atwood, Barbara Gowdy, and Ellen Gilchrist. "This is the story of a friendship," writes Victoria Jenkins, "about the fierce, deep ways girls love each other and how girls define themselves by what their friends are and they are not."[10] Carole Stabile sums it up in very similar vein: "This is a story about friendship, about the love that sustains two young women in spite of (or perhaps because of) the norms of femininity that threaten to divide them."[11]

The defining differences between Berie and Sils to which both these reviewers allude revolve around sex. Just as the adult Berie perceives herself as gauche and inelegant by comparison with stylish, sexy Marguerite, so, as an adolescent, Berie feels immature and unattractive compared with Sils. At the center of her negative self-image is her flat chest. In late childhood Sils and Berie were united in their fascination with breasts, fashioning artificial busts for themselves with everything from golf balls to teacups, poring over centerfolds and underwear advertisements, and even persuading Sils's mother to show them her "veiny, and dark, and amazing" bosom (14). By the age of fifteen, however, Sils's figure is well developed; her low-cut Cinderella costume at Storyland displays a cleavage that is the envy of Berie, whose own breasts are still no more than "two wiener-hued puffs" (13). Berie's response is to ironize her own deficiency by telling "long self-deprecating jokes" about fried eggs, pancakes, and bug bites (14).

Sils's sexual beauty is thus instrumental in Berie's process of identity formation, at least partly accounting for the kind of person Berie becomes. Since, for all her "personal rituals of assertion and disguise" (38) involving clothes, accessories, and makeup, Berie cannot hope to compete with Sils in terms of physical appearance, she creates an alternative identity for herself as Sils's witty sidekick. As Tom Shone puts it, through the story of the evolving friendship between the two girls, Moore shows where Berie's "smart-aleck tone . . . comes from, [and] what first caused the smart aleck to smart."[12]

Berie's wisecracking personality persists later, at Mount Brookfield School, where she adopts a "loud" dress style—black and gold, glittery and heavily accessorized—in opposition to the prevailing preppie culture but sends up her extravagance as "a joke, a put-on" (126). Mystified by her menarche, or rather, by the novel sanitary paraphernalia it entails, she is yet more disorientated by her eventual development of a bust, and experiences a temporary identity crisis that extends to a linguistic plane: "I didn't know who I was, what I looked like, what jokes to tell" (127). She resolves the problem by repeating her earlier stratagem of self-mockery and laughing her new breasts off as "knockers, blimps, hooters, bazooms" (127).

Numerous critics have commented on the physical intimacy and emotional intensity of the bond between Berie and Sils—a combination that leads Michael Griffith to identify Sils as Berie's "first love."[13] Commentators have not generally defined the relationship as specifically sexual, but Monica Fagan, in the most detailed published reading of *Frog Hospital* to date, interprets the two girls as incipient lesbians whose intimacy might culminate in sexual consummation if not for the pressure to date boys exerted on them by "patriarchal, heteronormative society."[14] It is true that Berie's descriptions of Sils linger on details of her anatomy—her eyes, skin, and hair (10); her veins, tendons, and "shimmery" nails (22)—and that some of these passages could be construed as expressions of repressed desire. At one point, for instance, Berie recalls how she "tried not to look toward [Sils's] breasts" (13). However, Berie's confessed obsession with breasts is attributable more to curiosity, envy, and disappointment than to sexual desire. She never speaks of wanting to touch Sils's bosom, and although relations between Sils and Berie are "laced," to quote Valerie Miner, with "erotic awakening," it is, as

Miner says, a "diffuse" awakening, particularly on Berie's part —and in Sils's case is directed unequivocally at the opposite sex.[15]

By her midteens Sils is sexually active, but throughout the closest phase of their friendship Berie remains presexual. Not until she goes away to school without Sils does she experience physical maturation and sexual initiation. Although, as Fagan points out, certain descriptions of her first lover, Howie, closely echo earlier descriptions of Sils (for example, the reference to the "delicate veins" in Howie's penis, 128), Berie's carnal desire for Howie represents a completely different "way of seeing" (to borrow a phrase from John Berger[16]) from her reverence for Sils's beauty. Howie arouses her first sexual hunger—a fierce, "animal," phallocentric desire, an "obsession" with Howie's naked body and its commingled "vulnerability" and "power" (128). The newly sexualized Berie also acquires a new self-consciousness as what Berger might term "an object of vision: a sight."[17]

> I developed a blush. Before then, I had never blushed. I didn't have the body fat, the heat, the hormones, the awareness of myself, the belief in my own visibility, that would have created a blush. But now I'd become a sexual creature with all its experience of shame and being watched . . . and I began to blush easily, daily. I blushed for years. (128)

Shared Language

Although Berie doesn't become sexually active until separated from Sils, much of their growing up is done side by side: through shared experiences, overlapping personal histories, and the common fabric of their everyday lives. In Fagan's words, "These two girls mature through interdependence and interconnectedness."[18] Looking back, Berie as middle-aged narrator recognizes this dependency, particularly as it applied to her: "Should I have been expected to create my own self, out of nothing, out of thin, thin air and alone?" (17). In isolation, this implies, Berie would have been incapable of personality formation and self-definition; she required social context and personal connection, both of which were furnished, during the Horsehearts years, primarily by Sils.

An essential feature of Berie's and Sils's relationship and self-fashioning is language. They speak in the same idiom—one composed of song lyrics, slang, slogans, and private jokes. It is sufficient for one of them to say offhandedly, "What the fuck, babe," to make the other "fall on the floor, convulsed with laughter" (15). Jokes (or, rather, nonjokes) like this operate mainly as acts of intimacy, affirmations of what the philosopher Ted Cohen calls "a shared outlook on the world."[19] Their success relies on common background; if the receiver does not have enough in common with the teller to laugh, the attempted joke is "asymmetrical" (32) and the ensuing silence produces a feeling of "estrangement" (26). In the case of a successful joke, by contrast, shared mirth forges a valuable human connection: "That we do it [laugh] *together* is the satisfaction of a deep human longing, the realization of a desperate hope. It is the hope that we are enough like one another to sense one another, to be able to live together" (29). When Berie and Sils laugh immoderately at each other's one-liners, they affirm exactly this sense of being "like one another." This is not to say that they are, or seek to be, identical in every respect but that the affinity between them—expressed as it is through ironic, elliptical communication, a sort of wisecracking shorthand—outweighs the disparities.

The girls' strong mutual identification also involves self-conscious differentiation from others. For instance, their frequent allusions to popular music culture—through titles of songs, names of bands, snatches of lyrics, and references to nightclubs and rock concerts—constitute a "cool" verbal currency that distinguishes them from unfashionable contemporaries, such as Berie's adopted sister LaRoue, and the older generation. To distance themselves from adults, above all adults whom they perceive as parochial, they use conscious verbal strategies —strategies that are frequently based on mimicry but have the paradoxical effect of signaling difference. When they employ verbal tags and silly phrases such as "Okey dokes, artichokes" (42), they are echoing speakers from social groups they regard as unsophisticated. They scare-quote their utterances in parodic ways, making fun of other speakers and thereby tacitly positioning themselves higher on the social ladder. Growing up as they do in the "hick" (93) town of Horsehearts, where respected personages use homespun words such as "cream de *mint*," "cheeseburgs," and—the ultimate colloquialism—"'bingo' for 'yes'" (113), mimicking this language is part of their project of setting themselves apart from and above provincial society.

Moore employs subtle techniques for conveying the girls' disdain for the various kinds of adult language in circulation in their society. Free indirect narration and an absence of punctuation convey boredom with a parental lecture about "staying out late and being generally inconsiderate what was it with us girls" (61), while the inanity of commercial language is expressed through the overuse of capital letters and the lack of punctuation in Berie's Storyland name tag: "Hello My Name Is Benoite-Marie" (10). The punctuation mark used most frequently for expressive effect is the exclamation mark. Here as throughout Moore's work it invariably signals irony, as when Berie scrawls "Yeah, right, Spiro Baby!" on her Spiro Agnew poster (49) or makes fun of *Seventeen* magazine's chirpy advice about how to prepare for a date in thirty seconds: "He's striding unexpectedly up the walk! What should you do? *Quick! Brush your hair and tie a freshly ironed kerchief around it!*" (49). In the second example the exclamation marks originate in the *Seventeen* article, but because the quotation is incorporated into Berie's narrative without quote marks, the voice seems to merge with hers and the exclamation marks appear to derive from her. Snippets of discourse from external sources—song lyrics, car bumper stickers, political slogans, jokes—are repeatedly imported into the narrative in this way, blurring the boundary between Berie's inner voice and voices from the surrounding culture. This is one of the subtle ways in which *Frog Hospital* "catalog[s] . . . the cultural paraphernalia of an era," as Moore would later put it in relation to Joyce Carol Oates's high school novel *Broke Heart Blues*.[20]

Linguistic relationships, then, are indispensable to Berie's self-development, and her most satisfactory sense of identity ("I wanted no other constructions," 140) is as the close friend of Sils, with whom, literally and metaphorically, she speaks the same language. Both before and after this, in early childhood and middle age, Berie is shown as isolated and dislocated in a "strange-tongued world" (140). She remembers the Carr family household as a polyglot environment where French Canadian and German were used by her mother and father respectively as "tense marital code, off-limits to the *kinder*" (7), while visiting students and academics spoke such a variety of foreign tongues that she was apt to confuse English words and phrases with foreign ones: "I believed Sandra Dee was not only an actress but one of the French days of the week" (7). Her linguistic disorientation in unhappy early life is replicated in unhappy later life, when, in Paris, she speaks to Daniel in a mixture of native and foreign tongues: "'Bye,' I say to him. '*Au revoir*'" (73). Although they still exchange wordplay and wisecracks, the mood is heavy hearted and there is a sense of overfamiliar formulae: "Or something like that. I say something like that" (47); "It goes like that. Our talk goes something like that" (48). At times the disintegration of their marriage is reflected, not in stale and weary talk, but in a retreat to despairing silence. When Daniel admits, in a whisper, that he fears he will end up leaving her, Berie's reaction is mute: "I say nothing" (144).

A Reluctant Pessimist

In an interview in 2002 Moore denied a charge of cynicism in favor of an admission of pessimism: "I am a reluctant pessimist—an only half-disabused romantic."[21] The overall mood of *Frog Hospital* is pessimistic, and Berie's cyclical life course, which starts and ends among people to whom she cannot talk, is a major facet of this. Her best chances of happiness seem all to be in the past, with people—primarily Silsby and Daniel—who "invaded" her heart, "inadvertently formed [her], then vanished" (17).

Michael Griffith attributes the melancholy mood of the novel to its preoccupation with the past: even Berie's happy memories, he finds, "are set into a framework that makes them resound with grief."[22] Because the narrative is overwhelmingly retrospective, and because we know that the narrator is now unhappy, "every detail in the book has a doubled, ambivalent message: we see the joy with which Berie invokes that 'unwed and fabulous and crazed' summer of anticipation, but it's a joy undercut by the knowledge that . . . narrative flourishes only after life has gone and happened." Griffith's analysis has much in common with autobiographical memory theory, according to which first-person reminiscence is highly susceptible to influence by an individual's "current emotional state."[23] Some theorists identify autobiographical memories as being created, rather than merely expressed, by the act of telling; as David C. Rubin puts it, they are "constructions that come into being as they are told."[24] In Berie's case the potentially creative value of the remembering process is reduced by her melancholy state of mind in Paris. She can narrate her memories of adolescence, but to do so is further to imprison herself in the past, and a question she poses toward the end of the novel acknowledges this: "What to do with all those years of one's life: trot around in them forever like old boots—or sever them, let them fly free?" (137).

The sense that Berie's future holds little prospect of fulfillment is compounded by the novel's ending, which takes the form of a backward glance. Recollecting a tenth-grade choir rehearsal, Berie describes how the sun streaming in through the windows of the school gym turned the girls into "something celestial," their voices "took flight," and in an ecstatic transcendence of the ego, individual identities merged to form a collective whole, "like a hyacinth" composed out of "separate rose and lavender mouths" (147). Even then Berie experienced this union through song as "a valedictory chorus to our childhood." Now, when all that is positive and meaningful in her life appears to be past, the note of valediction is overwhelming. "In all my life as a woman," she admits, "I have never known such a moment" (148).

The unlikelihood of a happy ending to Berie's story has parallels in other narratives embedded into the novel as allegories of the main plot. At Storyland, costumed as Cinderella, Silsby tries to make disabused romantics of the young visitors by debunking the message of salvation in the fairytale she represents: "There is no prince" (15). Comparable subversions are worked on another fairytale, "The Frog Prince," which is alluded to in the picture painted by Sils and named (after a real painting by Nancy Mladenoff) *Who Will Run the Frog Hospital?* The ambiguously costumed figures in the background of Sils's canvas may be "saints or nurses or boys or princesses," but the wounded frogs in the foreground have definitely not been transformed into handsome princes: they "looked like frogs who'd been kissed and kissed roughly, but stayed frogs" (18). Berie puts a feminist spin on this failure of transformation in another reworking of "The Frog Prince": a joke she tells Daniel about a woman who declines to bestow the transfiguring kiss because she is less interested in a prince than in a talking frog (70). This pointed joke implies an attack on Daniel, who has himself turned out a disappointing prince, but elsewhere a more sympathetic description aligns him with the bandaged or splinted frogs in Sils's painting: for all his failings, Daniel suffers in his way, and Berie perceives him as inhabiting "a place of woundedness" (146) beyond her sphere of solace.

Silsby's painting can be seen as one of the most significant allegories in this novel, since all of the main characters experience physical and/or psychological harm—Berie's fall, Sils's abortion, LaRoue's suicide, and even Mike Suprenante's motorcycle accident—and are therefore all casualties to a greater or lesser degree. The painting gives visual representation to the important idea of unremedied wounds, which is also encapsulated in another variation on the frog motif: the frogs maimed by BB pellets that Berie and Sils, as young girls, end up killing, not saving, with their well-intentioned amateur first aid (17). If, as Valerie Miner argues, one of the novel's principal themes is "the nature of caring,"[25] Berie's and Sils's inept ministrations to the injured frogs suggest a failure *of* care, while in other instances it is a readiness *to* care that is lacking. Berie, for example, is guiltily conscious of her unkindness to LaRoue in both adolescence and adulthood—a deficiency in affection that LaRoue's death puts beyond repair. As in its treatment of memory, so in its attitude to pain, this novel promotes a pessimistic message: that damage, once done, cannot be undone. A passage concerning Berie's abandonment of LaRoue at a 1970s rock concert brings together the two themes: "My cruelty toward her, now in me like a splinter, where it would sit for years in my helpless memory, the skin growing around; what else can memory do? It can do nothing: It pretends to eat the shrapnel of your acts yet it cannot swallow or chew" (58).

Conclusion

Berie's conviction that memory is "helpless" has significance for Moore's overall enterprise in writing *Who Will Run the Frog Hospital?* Like her first novel, *Anagrams*, this second novel investigates the process of constructing narratives and draws attention to fictional license. Berie's main story is narrated from memory, and as she concedes, "Things . . . stiffen and shift in memory, become what they never were before" (25). Whereas *Anagrams* foregrounds literary *potential*, however—the multiple possible ways of representing a life—*Frog Hospital* seems more concerned with the limitations and pointlessness of stories: not only does memory distort the past, but its distorted versions of events become fixed, stiffened, as difficult to dislodge as the splinter in the quotation above. Berie describes her past as having been summoned "by witchcraft—a whore's art, collage and brew, heart of horse, eye of newt" (25). The wordplay on the name of her hometown, Horsehearts, situates her extended flashback within this realm of witchcraft, aligning it with fairy-tale and implying that it has no more reliable relationship to— or utility in—the "real" world than a tale of the supernatural or a themed amusement at Storyland. Threaded through it are questions that reiterate ideas of impotence and missing agency, whether in relation to memory, history, or human caring: "What . . . can memory do?" (58), "Who will house the museum of museums?" (86), and the titular question, *Who Will Run the Frog Hospital?* If, from a metafictional perspective, questions like these can be read as casting doubt on the value of narrative, from a metaphysical perspective they imply existentialist crisis.

Birds of America

For a heady three-week period in October 1998, Lorrie Moore's third volume of stories, *Birds of America*, was ranked among the *New York Times* best sellers, shifting between fourteenth and fifteenth positions.[1] This was Moore's biggest book in terms of both sales and size. It was priced at twenty-three dollars and was nearly three hundred pages long—hefty enough, as she marveled in an interview at the time, to "keep a small door open."[2] The consensus among readers and critics was, and remains, that in this collection Moore also tackles her biggest themes. The month before it made the best-seller lists, a *New York Times* reviewer had described it as "her most potent work so far" and had praised one "powerhouse" story for having "the heft and ranginess . . . of a compressed novel."[3] Other reviewers followed suit: "Her depth of focus has increased, and with it her emotional seriousness"; her jokes "hit with an impact that leaves the reader stunned"; she "pushes further" than before "the extremes of emotional fragility"; her subject matter has "more complexity, substance, and gravitas."[4]

These plaudits are founded on *Birds of America*'s engagement with topics such as cancer, death, mental and marital breakdown, loneliness, and the love, lack, or loss of children—powerful themes, indeed, but themes that have informed every one of Moore's major publications from *Self-Help* onward. No one recalling the desolation felt by the deserted wife dying of cancer in "What Is Seized" or the mother's terror of losing her young son as well as her sanity in "To Fill" could claim that in *Birds of*

America "Ms. Moore . . . grapples, . . . as she has sometimes been reluctant to do in the past, with the real sadness and grief in her characters' lives."[5] *Birds of America* does address some of the darkest facets of human experience, but in doing so it continues a project in which Moore has been involved since her earliest publications.

James McManus sees sufficient homogeneity in *Birds of America* to label it "emphatically" a "cancer book."[6] This is understandable given that cancer makes several appearances in the collection and takes center stage in two of the strongest stories. But any unitary classification must understate the diversity of this volume. One of the most moving stories about terminal illness revolves around cystic fibrosis, not cancer, while others approach the theme of mortality from angles as different as accidental infanticide and the death of a cat. Nor is death or the fear of death the principal theme in every story. Most stories touch on it, but some are primarily concerned with other experiences: parent-child relationships, family lives, sexual love, travel, history, politics, American history, and the national character. The typology is complicated by the extent to which the categories overlap. For instance, the most famous story in the collection, "People Like That Are the Only People Here: Canonical Babbling in Peed Onk," is best known as a cancer story but could equally well be identified as a story about motherhood. To take another example, "Dance in America" could be viewed as only secondarily about disease and primarily about performance, transcendence, or the power of love.

Theaterstruck

In 2001 Moore told an interviewer that she had become "theaterstruck" at a very young age and that this relish for performance had filtered through into her work: "I suspect that love of

theater . . . is part of the pulse of everything I've ever written."[7]
Three stories about kinds of performer and performance—
"Charades," Willing," and "Dance in America"—provide an
illuminating route into *Birds of America* and introduce some
uses of the avian imagery. "Charades" and "Willing" explore the
role played by dramatization in identity construction and the
conduct of relationships, revealing the importance of theatrical
enactment to, respectively, a professional film actress and a family playing a parlor game at Christmas. In "Dance in America"
the focus shifts from the self-conscious staging of personality and
relationships to the value of unselfconscious performance.

"Charades"

Language is a central facet of all Moore's characters' senses of
self and relations to others, but in "Charades" the characters
play a game that substitutes movements and gestures for spoken
utterances. In this ritual Christmas pastime, words and their
meanings are translated into physical acts—acts, that is, in the
dual sense of actions and dramatizations. The main character,
Therese, and her mother, Marjorie, throw themselves into the
game both figuratively and literally, each performing physical
"pratfalls" that other characters find undignified or dangerous.
Their readiness to participate "gamely!" (96)—and the pun is
clearly intentional—is a physical counterpart to the wisecracking
impulses of many of Moore's most likeable protagonists: a
"good sight gag" (99) is an analogy for a good joke, with the
same need for an appreciative audience. This is provided for
Therese by her husband and teammate Ray, who is quick to
decode her gestures and, unlike her pedantic brother and sister,
does not argue about the rules. Ray's flexible and imaginative
approach to the game has parallels with his dyslexia, which

disrupts rigid systems of signification and produces inadvertent wordplay that he is self-deprecating enough to parody.

In some respects, however, the resort to acting in "Charades" is an admission of failure. The family imitate "a pack of thespians" because they have become estranged from one another over the years, to the point where Therese "no longer has any idea who Ann is" (99) and "hasn't a clue" (itself an allusion to the game) how to relate to Andrew (107). The negative meanings of the word "charade" come into play as the game disintegrates into an evident pretense at having fun and a travesty of an affectionate family celebration. Therese's cynical summary of the ritual Christmas proceedings—"everyone arrives, performs for one another, catches early flights out" (96)—is vindicated at the end of the story when an argument about racial prejudice and homophobia convinces her that it is time to leave for the airport. The year before *Birds of America* was published, Moore had written a humorous column about Christmas "performance anxiety" in her own household, but in that case the ritual festivities worked one of their usual "holiday miracles," producing a happy ending that the family in "Charades" fails to muster.[8]

"Willing"

While "Charades" is concerned with family breakdown among amateur thespians, "Willing" revolves around the nervous breakdown suffered by a professional. When her Hollywood career grinds to a halt, Sidra returns to Chicago and takes up residence in a Days Inn, where she experiences an identity crisis similar to those suffered by characters in *Like Life:* "There were moments . . . when she looked out at her life and went 'What?' . . . It had taken on the shape of a terrible mistake" (6). Some of Sidra's psychological problems originate in what she sees as her excessive willingness to be represented to the cinema audience as a sex object, through erotic shots of body parts such as naked hips or exposed shoulder bones. Yet the loss of this audience is the main cause of her collapse when she leaves Hollywood: the "life of obscurity" exposes "small dark pits of annihilation . . . in her heart," voids that were formerly filled by the habit of performance.

A relationship with an auto mechanic named Walter provides Sidra with fleeting opportunities for theatrical self-fashioning as Beatrice to his Benedick or as wife and mother in a domestic romance about "children and lawn mowers and grass clippings" (15), but the illusion is short lived. Walt's fatal deficiency as Sidra's lover is that he does not *see* her. He is unfamiliar with her films, falls asleep partway through watching one, and makes love to her with his eyes closed. Instead of freeing Sidra from the pressure of being viewed as an object, this blindness on Walt's part makes her feel erased or annihilated. Only with the discovery of Walt's infidelity does she recover her dramatic power, staging an indignant scene of confrontation and parting in which Walt is ill qualified to participate: "He should practice in a mirror, she thought. He did not know how to break up with a movie actress" (24).

It is at the point of resurrecting herself as an actress that Sidra is associated with birds: "She was . . . turning into something else, a bird—a flamingo, a hawk, a flamingo-hawk—and was flying up and away, toward the filmy pane of the window, then back again, circling, meanly, with a squint" (25). The transformation here is twofold, with the flamingo connoting flamboyant spectacle and the hawk representing penetrating observer: she is both object and subject, sees and is seen. The metaphor continues with a description of her departure—"She was gone, gone out the window, gone, gone" (25)—which reflects her escape from an imprisoning relationship with Walt and implies a future flight from the Days Inn and Chicago.

"Dance in America"

The most explicit use of bird imagery in connection with performance comes in "Dance in America," which begins by enumerating the metaphorical meanings of dance as the narrator, a peripatetic dance lecturer, sees them: "Dance begins when a moment of hurt combines with a moment of boredom. . . . It's the body's reaching, . . . the heart's triumph, the victory speech of the feet, the refinement of animal lunge and flight, the purest metaphor of tribe and self. It's life flipping death the bird" (47). Dancing is simultaneously corporeal and spiritual, a means of overcoming pain or boredom, affirming vitality, expressing both individuality and belonging. It is also, significantly, an articulate art form. The dancer's feet, like the players' hands and bodies in "Charades," are organs of silent speech; dance is a language in which steps do service for words.

One of the nonverbal meanings conveyed by dance, according to this passage, is defiance of death, since "flipping the bird" is a colloquial expression for an insulting gesture. This defiance reflects the narrator's general philosophy of dance, but it also has specific relevance for the situation she encounters in the story, in which a seven-year-old boy named Eugene has cystic fibrosis and is expected to die young. Eugene's exuberance—in spite of his illness—is evident in his rapt expression, shining eyes, exclamatory utterances, "singsong" voice (51), and reckless stunts that recall the pratfalls in "Charades." As he and the narrator watch a dance video together, she reiterates her belief in the transformative power of dance, "how movement, repeated, breaks through all resistance into a kind of stratosphere: from recalcitrance to ecstasy; from shoe to bird" (52). Again, the feet, here metony-mically designated by the word "shoe," are at the center of the imagined transformation, this time taking wing in an image that unequivocally associates birds with transcendence and rapture.

The force of the story, however, arises from the tension between this faith in the human power of overcoming and the all too recalcitrant fact of disease. For all the "magnificent and ostentatious scorn" (57) of Eugene's body when he improvises a dance of the planets after dinner, his premature death is in-evitable. This knowledge explains the narrator's anger when she returns to the idea of dance as a way of "speaking": "We say with motion, . . . This is what life's done so far down here; this is all and what and everything it's managed—this body, these bodies, that body—so what do you think, Heaven? What do you fucking think?" (57). The rage in this passage is directed at an unspecified deity ("Heaven"), but a pattern of references to ritu-als such as Lent, Fastnacht, and vespers suggests that its target is the Christian God.

The Specter of Death
"People Like That Are the Only People Here"

Organized religion is not the only institution that is attacked in "Dance in America." Eugene's father, Cal, makes an im-passioned speech about medical research funding that implies strong criticism of government priorities and uses the same obscene language as the narrator's outburst: "It's wonderful to fund the arts. It's wonderful; you're wonderful. The arts are so nice and wonderful. But really: I say, let's give all the money, every last fucking dime, to science" (49). This fury is something Cal has in common with the narrator in Moore's celebrated cancer story—and her most famous story to date—"People Like

That Are the Only People Here: Canonical Babbling in Peed Onk." Itself likely to become canonical following its inclusion in Richard Ford's bible of American short fiction,[9] "People Like That," like "Dance in America," combines metaphysical anger with antiestablishment protest, in this case directed at the medical profession. The narrator, a writer, strongly objects to the dehumanizing language used by medics treating her two-year-old son for a rare kidney cancer. Whether by employing jargon, making offensively offhand remarks, using tactless, ill-chosen diction, or indeed refusing to speak at all, the medical staff create a discursive environment that bears no relation to the family's intensely emotional experience.

In objecting to medical language (and an underlying institutional perspective) that she judges depersonalizing, and later in protesting against the summary delivery of anesthetic to the Baby, the Mother in "People Like That" joins a series of female characters in Moore's work who feel slighted or even violated by medical practice. Benna in *Anagrams,* Zoë in "You're Ugly, Too," and in this volume Ruth in "Real Estate" and Olena in "Community Life" all suffer what narratologist Katharine Young, in an analysis of medical discourse, describes as a "sense of the loss of self" at the hands of dispassionate medics.[10] In the Mother's case, it is both her son's and her own individuality that seems threatened by insensitive professional procedures. The use of generic names for all characters in the story—ranging from Mother, Baby, and Husband to Oncologist, Radiologist, and Surgeon—reflects the narrator's feeling that from a medical point of view theirs is a stock situation, and she angrily reminds staff that as far as the family is concerned, this is a unique emergency: "This isn't a 'kind of thing'" (235). Moore says she used impersonal labels for the characters "because I felt them to be caught in designated roles, as if in a script," even though—and this is the crux of the story—their distress "mocks the idea of a script."[11]

Like other medical narratives in which the focalizing character is the patient's mother, such as Amy Bloom's story about sexchange surgery, "A Blind Man Can See How Much I Love You," "People Like That" explores the interactions among relatives in the hospital waiting room.[12] This allows Moore to develop the tension between, on the one hand, the Mother's denial of parity between her son's illness and anyone else's, and, on the other, her reluctant acknowledgment that other children face comparable afflictions. The title "People Like That Are the Only People Here" introduces the idea of an environment structured around shared experience and characteristics, but the Mother resists identifying or empathizing with other parents in the same metaphorical boat—the "nightmare boat" (249) of pediatric oncology—and fantasizes about escaping: "Woman Overboard!" (250). Conflicting with this isolationism, however, is a need for solidarity. When one long-suffering father says, "I could tell you stories," she demands "the worst one" and is almost elated to discover that it concerns something that they too experienced (246). As with the idea of her family's crisis as a stock drama in which each of them plays a prescribed role, so with this notion of common narrative: the Mother both refuses and is forced to accept that life-threatening illness in children is fairly widespread and that other parents use storytelling as a coping mechanism just as she does.

The Mother's recourse to narrative is reluctant. Although her automatic reaction to discovering the first symptom of her son's illness is to demand a narrative explanation—"What is the story?" (212)—she repeatedly denies not only her own competence to write about infant cancer but the general amenability of such experience to verbal representation: "How can it be described?" (237); "This is a nightmare of narrative slop. This cannot be designed" (223). Nevertheless, a powerful narrative unfolds, albeit it in a disjointed form—some twenty-four sections over forty-eight pages—which she dismisses as "notes" (250). Given the parallels between the "real" and fictional worlds—a seriously ill toddler, a mother who is a professional writer and composes a narrative based on the experience—readers who focus on the autobiographical origins of this story cannot fairly be accused of what Moore has termed, in a different connection, "biographical overreading."[13] The personal origins of "People Like That," however, risk being a distraction from the broader implications of Moore's aesthetic choices. By structuring the story around the creative process of writing about illness (rather than around illness per se), Moore reaffirms her overriding interest in the centrality of language and narrative to the human sense of identity.

"Four Calling Birds, Three French Hens"

If "People Like That" attacks institutional medical practice, "Four Calling Birds, Three French Hens" takes a swipe—in more humorous vein—at psychoanalysis.[14] The main character, Aileen, is having difficulty coming to terms with the death of her cat, Bert, and resorts to visiting a bereavement counselor, Sidney, who dozes in his psychiatrist's chair while she tells tearful anecdotes about her deceased pet. The way that Aileen punctures her friends' attempts to unearth a "larger" meaning beneath her grief (111) suggests that the story may also be a dig at psychoanalytical literary criticism or other schools of deep textual analysis, at which Moore also pokes gentle fun in "Community Life."[15]

Underneath the comedy of "Four Calling Birds," however, lie serious concerns: with death, grief, sanity, and family love. Rightly worried about Aileen's grip on reality, Jack tells her, "I'm being earnest here. And not in the Hemingway sense, either" (113). A prominent critic has faulted this pun as gratuitous wisecracking, but like all Moore's wordplay it is subtly related to the narrative's underlying themes.[16] Jack's allusion to a famous author and notorious alcoholic reflects his belief that Aileen is losing contact with the real world because of her excessively literary orientation ("Their bookcase headboard was so stacked with novels and sad memoirs, it now resembled a library carrel more than a conjugal bed," 113) and her recourse to drink. Her morbid obsession and threatened breakdown are symbolized by the birds and other wildlife that take advantage of the cat's absence to invade the yard, and her eventual recovery is signaled when, on Christmas morning, she and her three-year-old daughter run around the yard scattering Bert's ashes and frightening the chickadees and squirrels out of the trees. If, in stories such as "Dance in America," birds are metaphors for irrepressible life, in "Four Calling Birds" they represent encroaching death. Thus according to the story's figurative scheme, for Aileen to join her family in celebrating Christmas by eating "the big headless bird" (121) is to reassert life over death—or, again, to "flip death the bird."

"Real Estate"

As discussed in chapter 3, Moore's earlier fiction about illness and mortality also draws on metaphors relating to invasion and infestation, but what is noteworthy in *Birds of America* is a tendency to displace the site of such intrusion to a dwelling. In "Four Calling Birds" Aileen's yard is colonized by "animal life" (113), in "Dance in America" there are raccoons in the chimney of Eugene's family home, and in "Real Estate" a new house purchased by a woman in remission from lung cancer is overrun with pests ranging from raccoons and squirrels to ants, cockroaches, bats, geese, and crows. The effect of this displacement is to present the dwelling place in question as a metaphor for the human body. In Ruth's case moving house is like trying to change bodies, and the vermin in her new property symbolize her inescapable disease. When Ruth discovers a teenage squatter ominously called Tod (a name that is also used for one of the young cancer patients in "People Like That"), the equation between parasitic invasion and death becomes explicit.

Ruth's response to the "proprietary" behavior of Tod is significant. Like Cal and the narrator in "Dance in America," the Mother in "People Like That," or Aileen in "Four Calling Birds" ("Anger to rage—who said she wasn't making progress," 113), Ruth reacts furiously to being confronted by the specter of death, ejecting Tod and his friends with a level of "bourgeois venom and indignation" (205) that shocks her. Her attitude to the other harbingers of death in her household is the same: she arranges insect poisoning, traps squirrels, kills unhatched goslings, beats bats to death, and buys a gun in order to shoot the crows. The use to which she eventually puts this gun—fatally shooting the final intruder into her house, a serial burglar named Noel—marks the culmination, and the end, of her fighting. Afterward she abandons herself to her resurgent disease, and fantasizing about "rising . . . through the air, floating out into a night sky of singing and release" (212), runs out of her house and disappears.

Motherhood

If the symbolism in "Real Estate" is among Moore's most overt, it is also some of her most polyvalent. Birds stand for both intrusion and escape; a house is variously a body, a marriage, and a heart; and a body, in turn, is a failed "temple," "a phone booth" (202), a prison akin to a zoo, the seat of death, and yet, paradoxically, also the fount of life. The female body's capacity for producing both unwanted and deeply desired organisms—tumors and babies—is the subject of a meditation on Ruth's part that links her to women throughout Moore's work: "It seemed her body, so mysterious and apart from her, could only produce illness. Though once, of course, it had produced Mitzy. . . . Mitzy was the only good thing her body had ever been able to grow" (203).

The mystery of motherhood is one of the consolations of material identity: the body is mutable but also miraculous, and death and birth, decay and regeneration are inextricably interlinked. Even so, as a self-centered young adult Mitzy is the source of little joy or comfort to Ruth, and thus joins a long line of Moore's fictional offspring (in particular, Ariel in "Places to Look for Your Mind") who are lost to their mothers. Whether through gradual distancing, outright rupture, physical or mental illness, or the death of one or other party, mothers and children in Moore's work are frequently divided from one another, and the centrality of the maternal bond to the women's self-concepts renders them disturbingly vulnerable to breakdown when this occurs. The examples of Ginny in "How to Talk to Your Mother" and Silsby in *Who Will Run the Frog Hospital?* suggest that, at least for some women, the most physically traumatic way of being parted from a child, through abortion, is also psychologically traumatic, leaving the woman concerned feeling haunted by the ghost of the terminated fetus.

"Terrific Mother"

In "Terrific Mother" Moore explores a related trauma: a young woman's accidental killing of a friend's baby. Her subsequent haunting by the dead infant takes psychosomatic form as an intermittent pressure in the crook of her arm or a sense of a toddler's presence behind her. Having not only caused death and bereavement but failed a test of "womanliness," Adrienne believes herself disqualified from motherhood and cast out from the mainstream, noninfanticidal society. "Normal life is no longer possible for me," she tells her boyfriend Martin despairingly (253).

Adrienne's exiled state—a virtually endemic condition for Moore's main characters, but here painfully magnified—is replicated in her trip to a study center in the Italian Alps, where Martin is a visiting scholar and she, having married him, is merely one of the spouses.[17] Intellectually marginalized by this lower status, she observes proceedings at the Villa Hirschborn with a satirical eye that frequently alights on the scholars' alien and pretentious language: their use of "words like *Heideggerian* and *ideological* at breakfast" (259), a musicologist's description of a composition as "fraudulent and replete" (256). Along with this academic jargon and affected diction, she is exposed to a barrage of Italian that compounds her sense of linguistic alienation and in turn her feeling of difference.

While the Italian setting of "Terrific Mother" dramatizes Adrienne's banishment from happiness and peace of mind (thus performing a similar function to Paris in *Who Will Run the Frog Hospital?*), the overseas trip also serves as both the occasion of and a metaphor for an emotional journey on Adrienne's part. Initially in a condition of guilt and anguish that affects her physiologically and sexually, she is healed by a Minnesotan masseuse named Ilke who says she once exorcised the demons from a haunted house. Various connected strands of imagery coalesce in the figure of Ilke. At times Adrienne perceives her fleetingly in the various guises of vampire, witch, confessor, God, or prostitute. Herself a sort of migrant American bird, she is most strongly associated with the white cockatiel that flies freely around her massage parlor, particularly through the "strong, small, bony" hands—"Leathered claws" (270)—with which she squeezes the tension out of Adrienne's body and gives Adrienne the sensation of becoming "a singing bird" (271).

Ilke is also figuratively associated with a midwife or mother: there are frequent references to her breasts and belly; at one point the narrator says, "She took hold of Adrienne's head and pulled" (270); and Adrienne explicitly identifies herself more than once as an infant or baby. Undergoing massage is thus comparable to rebirthing—not only for Adrienne, who emerges from the parlor with "her legs noodly, her eyes unaccustomed to the light" (282), but also for Martin, who has also received Ilke's services and is portrayed on the final page "curled inward" like a newborn, crying (291). Building on allusions to the Christian Nativity and the life of Jesus that punctuate the narrative, the story ends with a vision of the accidentally killed baby as an angel radiating absolution and forgiveness.

Compared with *Self-Help* or *Anagrams*, *Birds of America* is an unexperimental work, but there are a few unconventional features, such as the two pages in "Real Estate" covered with the exclamation "Ha!" (177–79), which Moore has described as Ruth's "scream."[18] Some stories include characters or incidents so freighted with symbolic weight that the realist framework has to bend a little in order to accommodate them. One such moment occurs in "Terrific Mother," when Adrienne lies naked on a hillside in a reverie on fertility, wisdom, and mortality from which she is woken by an old woman dressed in white who is identified as "the *guide*" (284) and likened to a witch. At a realist level she is a tourist guide conducting a visit to a ruined Roman fort, but her symbolic function is to "lead [Adrienne] back out into [her] life again" (284).

"Which Is More Than I Can Say about Some People"

The last motherhood story to be considered in this chapter, "Which Is More Than I Can Say about Some People," draws more strongly on ideas of magic, structured as it is around a mother's and daughter's pilgrimage to Blarney Castle in Ireland to kiss the magical Blarney Stone. The fabled power of that stone to endow those who kiss it with the gift of eloquent speech is linked to the story's theme, which can be summarized as Abby and Mrs. Mallon learning to talk to one another. Moore introduces this theme as early in her career as "How to Talk to Your Mother," and within *Birds of America* she alludes to it in passing in "Terrific Mother," when Ilke pronounces that the scholars at Villa Hirschborn "are overeducated and can no longer converse with their own mothers" (270–71). In "Which Is More Than I Can Say about Some People" Moore intensifies the need for cordial and meaningful communication between mother and daughter by presenting them confined together for long periods in a car.

Abby's main motivation for receiving the gift of the gab is so as to conquer her fear of public speaking in preparation for a new job. Until now she has composed intelligence-testing riddles for American Scholastic Tests, but her compositions have become too personal—"*blank* is to heartache as forest is to bench" (26)—and the organization is reassigning her to high school liaison. Her secondary motivation is temporary escape from both a husband who is "not a verbal man" (27) and an extramarital entanglement with a lyricist who is too verbal. Being accompanied by her mother is not part of Abby's original intention but is necessitated by her inability to drive a car with manual gears; Mrs. Mallon comes along not for the ride but to take the wheel, in an unmistakable dramatization of their relative positions of domination and subordination. The imbalance of power between them is consolidated by Abby's various fears: of flying, crossing the border into Northern Ireland, and traversing a rope bridge over a ravine. Intended as an enjoyable excursion and a purposeful quest, once hijacked by Mrs. Mallon the trip quickly acquires what Abby perceives as a "theme"—that "Abby had no courage and her mother did" (32)—and becomes a series of tests that Abby fails.

Always second in her mother's affections to her sister Theda ("sweet as ever, . . . which is more than I can say about some people," 29), Abby is subjected to a stream of disparaging and hurtful remarks that produce a regression to childhood: "I'm a child again, Abby thought. I'm back. And just as when she was a child, she suddenly had to go to the bathroom" (31). Enforced proximity to Mrs. Mallon triggers memories revolving around the physical maternal body and its natural functions, memories of bursting in on Mrs. Mallon in an unlocked toilet cubicle or being repelled by her greasy hair, her navel, and her soiled sanitary towels. A daughter's fear and disgust with regard to her mother's body is, again, traceable back throughout Moore's oeuvre, and is always linked to the problem of knowing the mother, divining her secret self. Lynnie in "What Is Seized" comes upon the unnerving spectacle of her mother seated on the toilet with the bathroom door wide open "like some obscene statue," and is so shocked at the sight that she tells her schoolfriend that this woman with her underwear coiled round her ankles may or may not be her mother.[19] Berie in *Who Will Run the Frog Hospital* has to "try not to feel repelled" by physical details such as her mother's stubbled armpits, and admits to being afraid of intimacy with Mrs. Carr, whether physical or emotional.[20]

Abby, however, does not flee from the truth about her mother. At Blarney Castle Mrs. Mallon scolds her daughter for hesitating to assume the painful, dangerous position required for kissing the legendary stone, but after Abby overcomes her fears and blows a "peck" at the "unhygienic" slab (43), Mrs. Mallon herself is clearly terrified when her turn comes, and this reverses the prevailing dynamic in the mother-daughter relationship. In a clumsy and undignified performance that reveals her underwear and necessitates the assistance of an attendant, Mrs. Mallon is exposed as vulnerable—a revelation that gives Abby new power and strength, so that it is she who leads the way back down the castle tower. With Abby's coat spreading out around her like a new pair of wings (44), this reverse progress down the dark stairwell resembles a birth or hatching. As with Adrienne's renascence on the massage table in "Terrific Mother," Abby experiences a remedial rebirthing, in her case repairing the damage caused by decades of maternal disparagement.

Under the influence of a "restorative" pint of Guinness at Brady's Public House (44), Abby takes advantage of her newfound confidence and eloquence by proposing an affectionate toast to Mrs. Mallon: "May you be with me in my heart, Mother, as you are now, in this place; always and forever" (46). The generosity of this tribute contrasts with Mrs. Mallon's ingrained verbal parsimony toward her daughter, but in lifting her pint glass in acceptance of the toast, she signals a willingness to follow Abby's lead and enter into a warmer and more open relationship. With this progression from tests to toasts, this story—like "Four Calling Birds," which also closes with a toast—thus ends on a note of optimism and renewal, the raised glass serving an analogous figurative purpose to a bird ascending or in flight.

On the Road: "What You Want to Do Fine"

By featuring two women as its travelers, "Which Is More Than I Can Say about Some People" joins American fiction such as Bobbie Ann Mason's *In Country* (1985) and Barbara King-solver's *Bean Trees* (1988)—as well as Ridley Scott's 1991 film *Thelma and Louise*—in feminizing the predominantly masculine motif of the road trip.[21]

Birds of America contains another road-trip story, "What You Want to Do Fine," which differs from masculine paradigms such as *On the Road* (1957) by presenting a gay, blind man and his bisexual, sighted traveling companion. The theme of transgressive sexuality links the story to Vladimir Nabokov's road-trip novel *Lolita* (1955), a text that Moore explicitly recalls by naming one of her travelers after a character in that novel: Quilty. Moore's Quilty shows a relish for puns and other forms of wordplay that is worthy of a Humbert Humbert, so that on one level the story can be read as a camp homage to Nabokov. Beyond its playful investigation of sexual emotions and morality, however, lie weighty themes such as warfare, American history, and the national character.

The historical tour taken by Quilty and Mack coincides with military buildup to the 1991 Gulf War, a conflict that the two men satirize as the "big George Bush showdown," "a sales demo for the weapons," and "a television show" (153 and 161). Quilty is unequivocally opposed to the impending war, believing that the senseless outcome of the operation will be an "incredible heartbreaking list" (156) of fatalities like the roster of Vietnam dead. Mack's position, as a former soldier, is more ambivalent, and comparison of "What You Want to Do Fine" with an earlier published version titled "Lucky Ducks" reveals numerous changes that emphasize this ambivalence.[22] Mack scolds Quilty for viewing the casualties in Vietnam too abstractly ("*Guys* died there. A list didn't die there," 156) and yet is sorry that his name is not among those on the Vietnam War Memorial in Washington, D.C.: "I'm jealous because—stupid me—I waited until peacetime to enlist" (156). He feels disgust for televised combat ("armies as TV-network football teams?") but "still believes in armies" (162), a caveat that distinguishes his attitude from Quilty's rigid antiwar stance.

Mack's regret at not having seen active service seems bound up with anxiety about his gendered identity. His sense of exclusion from the honorable fraternity commemorated in the Vietnam "buddy statue" (156) is associated with his feelings of compromised masculinity at having entered into a homosexual relationship with Quilty, and of weakness and shame at having succumbed to alcoholism, been left by his wife, and lost custody of his son. The cyst on Mack's penis, and the scarring that he fears may result from its recent removal, constitute imperfections in his embodiment of masculinity that operate as a metaphor for his—as he sees it—impaired manhood. Quilty, meanwhile, is at home in an effeminate homosexual milieu and aspires to no macho ideal of maleness. The two men's divergent sexual, educational, and cultural backgrounds are paralleled by their differing genealogies: Quilty is Jewish and Mack is Irish American. Furthermore, Quilty is a northern Yankee engaged in a temporary excursion to the South (and here the text employs explicit imagery of migrating birds, 161), while Mack's regional origins are in the more southerly state of Kentucky. These opposing affiliations come out at the Vicksburg cemetery, where Quilty performs a stagy encomium to the Hoosier dead while Mack "lets loose with an incongruous rebel yell" that prompts Quilty to ask him whose side he is on.

Vicksburg is one of several cemeteries on the men's present and past itineraries; others include Saratoga, Arlington, and Mother Goose's grave in Boston. Mack's private label for such sites is "the Bone Zone," a rhyme that is repeated more often in the final text than the original version to create a powerful linguistic consciousness of mortality. War is not the only cause of death overshadowing this story; AIDS also lurks in the background, and it comes to the fore when Mack and Quilty visit yet another cemetery for an AIDS funeral.

The incongruously recreational name of one of Tapston's cemeteries, Resurrection Park, is comparable to the trite names for heritage sites and tourist facilities that cash in on the literary history of the South, among them "the Mark Twain Diner, the Tom 'n Huck Motel," and a touring train that Quilty archly dubs "Too, Too Twain" (155). Such tourist attractions' flimsy claims to historic fame are epitomized in a site that Mack and Quilty visited on a previous trip, to Key West. This was a house that they initially understood to have belonged to the renowned nineteenth-century ornithologist John James Audubon, but that they subsequently learned was only somewhere he had once stayed. Further disillusionment came with the discovery that Audubon was a man of violence in his way: he shot the birds in *Birds of North America* before painting them. Ironically adopting this as a metaphor for the creative process in general, Quilty extends it to the embodiment of literary machismo, "Papa" Ernest Hemingway, who, he jokes, shot his characters before writing about them (157). Hemingway's house is another landmark that Mack and Quilty have visited—in this case wearing feather boas in order to "taunt" the writer's prized masculinity (157).

Along with an antebellum courtliness of speech that is more pronounced in the final than the first version of the story, this camp performance contributes to a construction of Quilty as theatrical and exhibitionist, an inveterate performer who declaims to his audience like "a goddamn Victorian valentine" (146). Nowhere are Quilty's melodramatic tendencies more pronounced than in the scene in the Peabody Hotel at the end of the story. Having included the renowned hotel in Memphis in their itinerary for the express purpose of watching the resident flock of tame ducks parade along a red carpet, Quilty upstages the birds by throwing himself at Mack's feet in a display of contrition for a fit of jealousy, and then graciously accepts the onlookers' applause, which is actually intended for the ducks.

Although Quilty's show of emotion is an attention-seeking performance, there is a sincere foundation to his periodic ritual of "audition[ing] for love" (176). As in all Moore's fictions, the search for stable and meaningful intimate relationships is a major theme here. In the metaphorical terms set up by the story, Mack and Quilty are less comparable to the privileged Peabody ducks (the "Lucky Ducks" of Moore's original title) than the nomadic "mange-hollowed hawks, . . . lordless hens, . . . dumb clucks" who "will live punishing, unblessed lives, winging it north, south, here, there, searching for a place of rest" (174). America as represented in this image is a difficult habitat—the site, as the use of the future tense indicates, of indefinitely fruitless questing.

In relation to other constructions of America within this narrative (America as military superpower, as heroic battlefield, as proud possessor of a virile literature and a noble history), Mack and Quilty are poised between detachment and investment, skepticism and faith. Touring their country provides an opportunity to observe and comment on symbolic details of the culture, including baseball (165), "musical comedy" (162), McDonald's (158), and Coca-Cola (166). Sometimes humorously affectionate in tone, but more frequently marked by derision, especially on Quilty's part, their commentary forms a droll metanarrative of Americanness.

To the extent that America is presented as the scene of difficult and painful searches for love, however, Mack and Quilty are portrayed as typical citizens—very much in and of their national milieu. An America characterized by transience, absence, and loss emerges as their inescapable environment. The missing-child posters to which Mack is drawn at several points in the narrative illustrate a lamentable feature of the social fabric: the community's failure to protect its most vulnerable members. But they also have personal relevance for Mack, whose son Lou, now living with Mack's estranged wife Annie, is as lost to him as the abducted, murdered, or runaway five year olds in the pictures (161, 164). Comparison of "What You Want to Do Fine" with "Lucky Ducks" reveals that the revised text more explicitly links Mack and Quilty to the missing-child posters and thus to the national malaise these encapsulate. In New Orleans, milling among crowds of medical-convention delegates after cruising on the river in an old-fashioned paddle wheeler, Mack sees more posters of missing children. "Lucky Ducks" proceeds to give the children's names and ages, but "What You Want to Do Fine" includes an extra sentence that projects Mack and Quilty into the national picture: "He half-expects to see himself and Quilty posted up there, two more lost boys in America" (170).

The American Way
"Community Life"
The word "missing," with its various connotations of yearning, pining, losing, lacking, and overlooking, appears in "What You Want to Do Fine" seven times and has resonance for the tone of the story as a whole when Quilty says wistfully, "Missing is all I do" (161). The same verb is prominent in another story that engages explicitly with American national identity, "Community Life." Here Romanian-born Olena, who was raised in Vermont and now lives in the Midwest, misses many things—her late parents, her home country, and her native tongue—but as a refrain emphasizes, "She missed her mother the most" (76). The reshuffled letters of Olena's name spell "alone," encapsulating the isolation she experiences in America, for all her late parents' earnest wish that she should "blend into" American society (58) and her boyfriend's insistence that she "get involved in the community" (74).

The principal theme of "Community Life" is precisely what it means to belong, and contribute, to the American community. Robert Bellah and colleagues address this and related questions ("How ought we to live? How do we think about how to live? Who are we, as Americans?") in their enquiry into middle-class Americans' conceptualizations of a moral and purposeful life.[23] Their interviewees valued personal freedom above all other attributes, but associated this freedom with "participation in local politics" and "a connection to a wider political community" (vii). A reiterated call among these interviewees was "get involved!" (167), and this led the authors to report that the "United States is a nation of joiners" (167).

In "Community Life" the urge toward involvement and participation is sharply satirized through the character of Nick, campaign manager for a county board candidate and a vociferous proponent of "the American way" (74). Nick's self-promotion as good citizen is undercut by repeated references to his evasive gaze and a quality "like pond life" in his eyes (61), which, together with his sexual infidelity to Olena, construct him as a shifty and self-interested opportunist. His fellow activists, drawn from the "local leftover Left," are equally incapable of sincere connection: "They never really spoke *to* you. They spoke toward you. They spoke at you. They spoke near you, on you" (66). By combining prepositions that connote incomplete proximity ("toward," "near"), aggression ("at"), and violation ("on"), this passage evokes the dual experiences of isolation and assault that emerge as the predominant terms of Olena's relation to American society. Her unhappiness and insecurity are reflected even at the level of word games known as Tom Swifties that punctuate the narrative: "*She's a real dog, he said cattily*" (74); "*You're only average, he said meanly*" (75). She becomes "afraid" of the community (70), declares that she hates her adoptive country (74), and ends the story in a dispossessed condition for which—aptly, since she works as a librarian—she finds a literary analogy: "She had lost her place, as in a book" (77).

"Agnes of Iowa"

If "Community Life" narrates an immigrant's experience of remaining an outsider, "Agnes of Iowa" revolves around a character who strongly identifies with America. Agnes is a native of Cassell, Iowa, who, after an unsuccessful experiment in living in New York, makes her adult life in her birthplace, where she demonstrates her commitment to the public good by teaching a

"Great Books" night class and doing volunteer work on the Transportation Commission. By attaching name to place, the title of the story establishes this affiliation: Agnes is *of* Iowa; she comes from there; she belongs there. During her New York phase, however, she uses the French spelling of her name (Agnès, pronounced "On-yez") as part of the reinvention of herself as more "intriguing" (79).

Part of the fictional enterprise here, as in "Community Life," is to satirize naïvely politicized behavior. Agnes's youthful gestures at protest include taking a half-hearted feminist stand against normative ideas of feminine beauty ("basically: she shaved her legs, *but just not often enough*," 84) and signing petitions in support of both abortion rights and free day care. Both these issues can be regarded as pertaining to women's freedoms, but Agnes's stance is ill thought out, as references to her twenties as her "mishmash decade," "messy with contradictions," imply (79).

The main storyline concerns Agnes's automatic hostility to a visiting Afrikaner poet on the grounds that he is a white South African. Her position on racial identity has already been exposed as unthinking by a black creative writing student, Christa, who believes that Agnes has for her an "Alice Walker and Zora Hurston" agenda of black consciousness and political commitment (82). Despite belonging to the racial group oppressed under apartheid, Christa is friendlier to the white South African poet than is Agnes, whose first impressions and responses to him are conditioned by his (in her opinion) indefensible allegiance to "*that country. . . .* How could he live in that country?" (86).

When Beyerbach emerges as a liberal opponent of apartheid and an advocate of free speech, Agnes revises her view of him, both in literal terms (she sees his appearance as more attractive when she is "standing up close," 89) and in the sense of how she judges his moral and political nature. But her new image is not much more proof against distortion than her original misconception; she falls slightly in love with him, but it becomes painfully clear that the feeling isn't mutual when he bids her a commonplace farewell: "All best wishes to you" (91).

"Beautiful Grade"

In "Agnes of Iowa" Agnes's initial indignation at Beyerbach's residence in South Africa during apartheid is mirrored by an equivalent challenge to her own national loyalty during the Vietnam War. She recalls a Danish person asking her to defend the fact that she lived in the United States at this time, and remembers that she replied: "A lot of my stuff is there" (88). This ostensibly flippant answer produces a comic effect through deflation, but it contains a truth about the nature of people's attachment to their native states, even when they oppose or question those states' policies. This issue is at the heart of the last story to be discussed in this chapter, "Beautiful Grade," which dramatizes a clash of perspectives on World War II and Vietnam.

Writing about *Birds of America* in the *Yale Review,* Michael Frank notes that several of the stories are structured around what he calls a "time-out," that is, an excursion from characters' normal routines and locations.[24] In the case of "Beautiful Grade," though Frank does not explicitly make this observation, the "contained, . . . contain*able* interlude" is a dinner party that places Serbian and German guests at an American table and thus provides a platform for heated expressions of competing political allegiances and national loyalties. Both Frank's review and a piece written by James Urquhart omit this concern with war, atrocity, and complicity.[25] Urquhart justly praises "Moore's delineation of each diner's meagre powers of empathy" with the main character, Bill, in respect of his personal relationship with a former student; what he overlooks is the assorted guests' similar inability to identify with one another's political feelings.

The discord begins when Lina, an expatriate Serb, introduces the subject of national identities by insisting that her son is "a total *sairb*" even though his father, Jack, is American (125). The national pride underlying this assertion also emerges in the derision she expresses for Serbia's historic enemies within the former Yugoslavia. Her disparaging quip about Yugoslavians who attend college courses in waitering skills provides a cue for equally belittling witticisms on other diners' parts about the penchant of Japanese people for committing street crime and reprogramming computers, so that for a time the conversation degenerates into an exchange of national stereotypes—though the guests assure themselves that they are not being racist "in any real way" (128).

In this story, as throughout Moore's oeuvre, however, verbal acts such as jokes are inescapably "real," if less directly harmful than physical actions. A further illustration of this is the fierce criticism Lina attracted in Belgrade, in a period prior to the story's events, for speeches made on local radio. Her references to "fascist Croats" and the dangers of "a nationalist, Islamic state" provoked retaliation, also in the verbal mode, as students picketed her office with signs that challenged her perspective: "GENOCIDE IS NOT 'COMPLICATED' and REPENT, IMPERIALIST" (131).

The focus on the verbal and the textual as political acts continues in Bill's recollections of a telephone conversation between him and Lina following the controversial interview. Characterizing herself as "a pacifist and resister" (131), she cited radio broadcasts and rock concerts she helped organize in opposition to Serbian policy, and her participation in a protest demonstration under Slobodan Milošević's window. The lameness of the slogan the protesters chanted, "Don't count on us" (131), was contrasted by Bill with the rhythmic mantra of anti-Vietnam protest: "Hell no, we won't go" (131). Although, then, both characters identified themselves as dissenting citizens, patriotic feeling nevertheless underpinned a competition between them concerning the effectiveness of their respective protest campaigns.

Another incident from the story world's past is a gathering of the same group of friends at which the conversation turned to World War II. Lina, who lost three uncles at the hands of the Nazis, was incapable of sympathy for Brigitte, an émigré German who was a little girl living in Berlin when the Allies bombed it. Irreconcilable private griefs and competing national allegiances placed the two women in opposed, and entrenched, positions. Meanwhile Bill, as onlooker, was preoccupied with the incongruously public context for Brigitte's display of private emotion. Her anguish shocked him partly because it was so intense "after so many years" but primarily because she broke down "over dessert . . . *at dinner*" (129).

If, on that earlier occasion, Brigitte transgressed a social code by being overly emotional, at the present dinner party Stanley (whose surname, Mix, points up his status as a galvanizing element in the social mixture) represents the opposite extreme: reprehensible neutrality. Pursuing a purely scientific interest in World War II, he travels regularly to Japan, where he is studying the "zoological effects" of radiation at Hiroshima and Nagasaki. His lack of attachment to place is reflected in the air miles he accumulates as a frequent flyer; he stands for liminal and unrooted agency, capable of being transferred, transported, and transplanted.

Stanley provokes Lina's moral outrage with his dehumanizing talk of "small-head-size data" (129) and his casual reference to the different types of bomb, one uranium and one plutonium, whose long-term effects he is engaged in researching. By participating in what now seems to have been planned from the outset as an atrocious experiment, he assigns himself a role in history that may be *a*moral in his view, but in hers is *im*moral. Committed to a rational epistemology, Stanley counters Lina's attack by calling into question her knowledge of history, advising her to improve her understanding of events in Japan by reading some of the "very good books . . . on the subject" (130). When she dismisses this suggestion, however, he resorts to more personal tactics directed at her national pride: as a Serb, he reminds her, she can hardly "take the moral high ground" in "a matter of foreign policy" (130).

In the background to these arguments lie Bill's meditations on free speech and the American Constitution. Since the latter defines the form of government in the United States, the role of its political institutions, and the rights of its citizens, it has almost metonymical status. To refer to the Constitution is to invoke America itself as a free and democratic society. By extension, to ironize the Constitution is to open up a humorously subversive perspective on the sacred foundations of that society, so that Bill's advocacy of a flexible, pragmatic, and evolving interpretation of the Constitution ("a blessedly changing thing," a "palimpsest" or "figmentary contract," 132) amounts to his mocking its generally revered authority.

The First Amendment, enshrining among other things the principle of free speech, functions as an especially powerful metonym in American culture. Bill, whose name can itself be seen as a pun on the Bill of Rights, is ready to topple even this icon. He expresses a willingness to sacrifice certain "First Amendment privileges," though all of them protect rights for which he feels political or cultural distaste in the first place: abortion protest, telemarketing, and pornography (132). In return for this relinquishing of unwanted freedoms Bill proposes a radical "gutting" of the Second Amendment. This violent verb contains a sly reflection of the amendment's provisions, which confer on the people the right to keep and bear arms and assert the security need for a well regulated militia. Bill's imagined bargain, by postulating—however jocularly—an infringement of verbal liberty in exchange for the curtailment of military entitlements, represents a further expression of the antimilitarism that pervades this narrative through the repeated references to World War II, the Balkans conflict, and especially America's war in Vietnam. An exchange between Bill and Lina underlines the centrality of the Vietnam War and protest movement to the collective American psyche and employs plural first- and second-person pronouns to emphasize Bill's inclusion in and Lina's exclusion from the American national identity: "'We *stopped* the war in Vietnam.' 'Oh, you are all so obsessed with your Vietnam,' said Lina" (132).

Conclusion

The dinner-party setting of "Beautiful Grade," by combining individuals from a variety of national and political backgrounds, presents what Bill, composing an essay in his head, thinks of as "*a paradigm of society*" (134). "What You Want to Do Fine," in similar vein, might be described as recounting a short tour in American military and literary history, or "Community Life" and "Agnes of Iowa" as offering snapshots of political (in)correctness and identity politics. These are stories, in other words, with clear intentions of encapsulating representative aspects of

American national life, and this overt interest in the nation's demographics, ideologies, and mythologies vindicates the last two words in the collection's title: *of America.*

The critical literature to date has overlooked this aspect of Moore's midlife volume. The title of Anita Brookner's review, "The Way We Live Now," creates an expectation that she will go on to discuss the narratives' various strategies for national portraiture—what it is that makes "these tales," in her words, "resolutely American"[26]—but in the event her commentary is confined to private dilemmas and disappointments. Her promising diagnosis of "millennial unease" among Moore's characters arises only from her feeling that no one in the book "is genuinely happy or spontaneous" rather than being linked to the stories' engagement with America's dubious past, imperfect present, and uncertain future. In enumerating the various inflections and applications of avian imagery in *Birds of America,* critics have missed one metafictional permutation, namely, the volume's own status as a bird's eye view of the nation.

CHAPTER 7

Other Works

At the time of writing her Gulf War story, which was published first as "Lucky Ducks" and then as "What You Want to Do Fine," Lorrie Moore could not have foreseen the events of September 11, 2001, which would ultimately lead the United States into a second armed conflict with Iraq. Nevertheless, between March and October 1998 she made editorial emendations that intensified that story's sense of the human costs of war. With hindsight these revisions seem to anticipate the overt antimilitarism of her story about the Iraq War, "Debarking."[1]

In the weeks and months immediately following the terrorist attacks on the World Trade Center and the Pentagon, many of Moore's peers were moved to produce fictional responses like the 110 pieces anthologized by Ulrich Baer or articles concerning the challenges and responsibilities facing writers in a world, as Jay McInerney described it, "forever altered."[2] Don DeLillo articulated a widespread view when he asserted the "singularity" of 9/11 and the need for new modes of "counternarrative" to balance the terrorists' hijacking, not only of four hapless aircraft but also of the national imagination.[3]

Whether out of a consciousness that the mass indiscriminate killings on September 11 had only too many antecedents in human history, not least the atom bombings remembered in "Beautiful Grade," Moore did not join the chorus of voices describing 9/11 as unprecedented. Her steadfast stance on the role of literature was quoted in the introduction to this book:

"Fiction has the same responsibilities after September 11th that it had before: and that is not to lie."[4] This is not to say that she was insensible of the physical and psychological impact of the targeted crashes. On the contrary a review of what she calls "the subtlest September 11 novel yet written," Peter Cameron's *Someday This Pain Will Be Useful to You* (2007), reflects her sensitivity to the profound damage that the sudden intrusion of "terrible violence" did to the "sense of safety in the world" of those involved—above all, the children.[5] The symbolic meaning of 9/11 is not, from this perspective, that America is outrageously vulnerable to assault by its enemies but that all humanity is equally exposed to "nonsensically brutal" adult violence.[6]

Moore's first work of fiction on 9/11 and the war on terror appeared in December 2003, nine months after the U.S.-led invasion of Iraq and seven months after President George W. Bush prematurely announced "Mission Accomplished."[7] Like her story about the first Gulf War, "Debarking" portrays domestic, civilian dissent to American war in the Middle East, taking military preparations—and in this case the homeland propaganda offensive—as its starting point. As in "What You Want to Do Fine," a doomed sexual relationship between a Jew and a gentile (here female) from Kentucky runs parallel to the international struggle. A relationship between a Jewish and a Catholic man is also reprised in this story, in the form of Ira Milkin's friendship with his colleague Mike. Both men are explicitly presented as opposed to the invasion of Iraq, and both show heavily ironic and strongly satirical tendencies. However, they are not constructed as anti-American figures; their investment in U.S. national culture and heritage is symbolized by the fact that they work for the State Historical Society in one of the "heartland" states.[8]

"Debarking" starts in the Christian festival of Lent 2003—a season in which Mike says mordantly that instead of fasting "we're giving up our democratic voice and our hope" (24). Criticism of the military campaign is expressed in references to "those . . . who are about to be blown apart by bombs" (24), while on the home front there is derision concerning chemical-weapons scares and makeshift defenses recommended by Homeland Security involving plastic sheeting and duct tape. Like many intellectuals in the United States, Moore is disturbed by the nationalistic lexicon associated with the war on terror. "I find very alarming the use of the word 'homeland,'" she stated in 2002, though with the important proviso that she was not "excusing or privileging anyone else's propaganda over ours": "I'm a little astonished when people do that."[9] In 2008 she elaborated her concerns about manipulative rhetoric: "When you have a war trumped up with falsehoods and propaganda the language that proceeds from it, and continues to narrate it, also perpetuates that original dishonesty. Terms are invented; euphemisms deployed; candor corrupted; language is made generally to conceal rather than reveal."[10]

In "Debarking," supporters and opponents of the invasion of Iraq deploy language visibly through channels such as bumper stickers and signs in their yards or at traffic intersections. Ira's young daughter Bekka deconstructs some of the popular discourse of protest: "'War Is Not the Path to Peace,' she read slowly aloud. Then added, 'Well—duh'" (43). The effect of this debunking is not to discredit the antiwar movement but to underline the counterproductive consequences of retaliatory violence: it may be self-evident to an eight-year-old child that war is not conducive to peace, but the adults in charge of the weapons apparently don't get it. By converse means but with the same effect of exposing politicians' dangerous belligerence, elsewhere Bekka disputes the logic of an antiwar slogan:

> "War Is Not the Answer," she read on another. "Well, that doesn't make sense," she said to Ira. "War *is* the answer. It's the answer to the question 'What's George Bush going to start real soon?'" (44)

Bekka's precocious power of interpreting war-related discourse is acquired in spite of, not thanks to, her private education. At her school "the students and teachers were assiduously avoiding talk of the war" (50). But as the story shows, "talk of the war" is common currency, permeating the public culture and seeping out into the private sphere.

If the coming war has a prominent linguistic presence in Ira's community, militaristic verbal formulations also mediate his fraught private life. His recollections of receiving divorce papers from his then wife (now ex-wife) Marilyn are framed in phrases specifically linked with two aspects of the U.S.-led offensive on Iraq in March 2003. The phrase "now, *there* was shock and awe for you" describes his reaction to being served the papers but alludes unmistakably to the military strategy for rapid dominance in Iraq; while the elaboration on his feelings, "there was *decapitation*," borrows the well-known term for the personal targeting of President Saddam Hussein (43).

Discourse associated with the war also infiltrates the narrative concerning Ira's short-lived sexual relationship with a pediatrician named Zora whom he meets at Mike's. At a verbal level, there is a dissonance between Zora and Ira from the outset—a dissonance that Ira experiences most painfully in a postcoital exchange in which Zora asks whether he managed to "get off" (36). The tasteless colloquialism conjures up an image of getting off a plane and brings to Ira's mind the word "debarking," which in turn anticipates his eventual disengagement from the relationship with Zora, as well as alluding to the disembarkation of troops in the Middle East and Ira's unwillingness to be "on board" that military operation.

Increasingly as the relationship progresses, Zora's words or actions do violence to Ira's feelings, in parallel with the developing violence in Iraq. At a time when Ira is too disturbed by news footage of the bombing of Baghdad to switch on his TV, Zora insists they go to an Arnold Schwarzenegger movie, which Ira finds "brutish" (45). Soon after this Zora reduces Ira to tears by telephoning to terminate the relationship (itself a Schwarzenegger-style maneuver), then reveals the extent of her insensitivity by shouting, "April Fool's!" (46), one of many thoughtless acts that make Ira feel "as if he'd been struck" (47). Language normally employed with reference to the so-called war on terror is applied to his need for protection from this kind of harm: "Strong international laws" should proscribe sexual allure in unbalanced people, he reflects. "The public's safety was at risk!" (47).

The analogy in "Debarking" between the public and private waging of war is continued in "Paper Losses," which revolves around marital breakdown between two middle-aged members of the "Make Love, Not War" generation: "Although Kit and Rafe had met in the peace movement, marching, organizing, making no-nukes signs, now they wanted to kill each other. They had become, also, a little pro-nuke."[11] The slow attrition of marital love is among the perennial themes in Moore's fiction and surfaces in her nonfiction writings. An essay on Shakespeare mentions "the low miserable hum of marital discontent" and a review of Updike identifies marriage as an "institution" whose "inmates" are doomed to a "condition of bruised pre-exile."[12] In both articles Moore's observations seem to have a bearing on the world outside as well as inside the literary works in question. As she states with unambiguous extraliterary reference in a review of Alice Munro, the death and "dismantling" of erotic love are ubiquitous experiences.[13]

While many of Moore's narratives chart a slow, melancholy distancing and disconnection between lovers, "Paper Losses" is notable for the bitterness and rage it attributes to failed marriage. The first paragraph uses the word "hate" three times—as a noun denoting an entity that Kit and Rafe have "spawned and raised." Rafe (whose name recalls "strafe" and thus evokes the idea of targeted attack) is the last in a series of unfaithful spouses in Moore's fiction to date—a husband, like Terence in "Real Estate," so radically altered that he seems to have "turned into some sort of space alien" (4). His disturbing hobby of constructing model military rockets in the basement, totems of phallic aggression and the male capacity for "horrifying violence" (10), dramatizes this estrangement.

A paragraph added to "Paper Losses" for its reprinting in *The Collected Stories* drives home the fact that Kit's and Rafe's marriage is "irretrievably broken" by reiterating that phrase three times (7). Initially unable to accept that the rupture is final, Kit insists on a previously booked family holiday to the Caribbean, but the condoms and candles she takes along go unused, and the only masculine comfort she receives is from a masseur symbolically named Daniel Handler (shortened to Dan in the revised version), whose ministrations arouse a mixture of "mad joy" and "bittersweet tears" (10). In "Terrific Mother" a masseuse is instrumental in Adrienne's psychic recovery and the regeneration of her sexual love with Martin, but in "Paper

Losses" there is no such happy ending. A metafictional coda looks ahead to a time when Kit would "tell this story differently, as a story, [and] would construct a final lovemaking scene" (12), but her actual experience is of the irreparable loss of love and even of the memory of love.

This closing idea of Kit's and Rafe's union as "past imagining" (12) helps explain Moore's use, as the title of the story, of a fiscal phrase for the loss of assets that have never been realized—possessions that were, in a sense, nonexistent in the first place. Grief for love that never really was is a universal experience for Moore's characters, perhaps most eloquently described by Benna in *Anagrams:* "All of life seems to me a strange dream about losing things you never had to begin with."[14] "Paper Losses" is also a pun on the unexpected divorce papers that Rafe (recalling Ira's wife in "Debarking") directs at Kit like a weapon, but its financial meaning is more obvious, and by framing her title in these terms Moore points to the political concerns that permeate this narrative: disapproval of a class of affluent ex-hippies who take expensive holidays on a "white, white, beach" (9) in "the colonial sun" (8), read books about genocide in Rwanda or Yugoslavia to assuage their consciences, and try "not to notice the dark island boys on the other side of the barbed wire" (9).

This is not the first expression of Moore's disgust with the Caribbean-going American middle classes. In a review titled "Patios & Poolsides" she commends Matthew Klam's attacks on precisely this moneyed group in his short-story collection *Sam the Cat and Other Stories* (2000).[15] Having denounced the "toxicity of American affluence," she ends with a warning about the divisive effects of economic disparity that on a post-9/11 reading seems chillingly prescient:

In the end [Klam's] book is a reminder that the wealth of the American upper middle class, and the suburban materialism of its lifestyle, is not old news, already sufficiently taken up by literary writers of previous decades. In the excessive ways it is experienced now, American affluence is unprecedented, socially and globally isolating in a manner that is new, overwhelming, and sinister to those looking on.

In the 2000 presidential election her sense of growing and dangerous inequalities between social—and especially racial—groups led her to vote for Ralph Nader, and later she speculated how differently history might have turned out if he had won: "One wonders whether 9/11 would even have happened with an Arab-American in the White House. I know it sounds naïve, but I don't think it is."[16] The same desire for a unifying president is evident six years later in an op-ed piece that subtly resonates with "Paper Losses." Discussing the merits of the two main candidates for the 2008 Democratic presidential nomination, she comes out in support of Barack Obama over Hillary Clinton on the grounds that he is a more inspiring symbol for the gendered and racial group in the United States who are most in need of leadership and support: "boys of color."[17] Recalling the image of the "local boys" debarred entry to the sphere of white privilege in "Paper Losses," this phrase also fits a pattern of references to the vulnerability of boys that can be traced back through "What You Want to Do Fine" and "People Like That Are the Only People Here" to "Places to Look for Your Mind." A few months before the 2008 presidential election, she reiterated her faith in Obama as a role model: "I am the mother of an African American boy and the import and impact of a candidate like Obama cannot really be overstated for kids."[18]

In "Paper Losses" Kit's son Sam is sensitive and needy, a cherished possession who under shared custody will soon—adding another meaning to the title "Paper Losses"—"float off and away like paper carried by wind" (8). This image connects Sam to the lost boys in, for instance, "Places to Look for Your Mind" and "What You Want to Do Fine," as well as to the fenced-out Caribbean boys in "Paper Losses," exiles in their own land. By contrast with Sam, Kit's daughters are "tough beyond her comprehension," armed with "Montessori code words" (9) and in full command of an educational system that Moore identifies in "Last Year's Role Model" as designed, "starting in kindergarten, . . . by and for white girls." This article describes American schooling as "a form of exile" for black boys, directly echoing Moore's language in an interview in which she pointed to a dominant feminine culture in U.S. classrooms and said that "a boy can feel exiled from that."[19]

Moore made this last remark in explicit connection to her son, Ben, and there is a suggestion that she was thinking of boys like him in writing "Paper Losses." As she has observed, "Writers write from what is on their minds."[20] This should not lure readers into either the biographical fallacy of scouring the work for clues to the life or its psychoanalytical corollary, what she calls the "therapeutic fallacy," which suggests that "writers are cathartically working out their problems in their writing."[21] Rather, in making links between personal circumstances and wider social phenomena, Moore's fiction and nonfiction illustrates her theory of history as operating through the "intrusions" into individual private lives of "the doings of the outside world."[22] The experience of having a mixed-race son and belonging to a family (Gentile, Jew, and African American) that constitutes, in her word, a multicultural "improvisation" personalizes social ills such as racial discrimination and the unequal distribution of opportunity.[23] Following the "awful presidency" of George W. Bush, and before that a Clinton era in which children from Baghdad to Waco "were appallingly killed," by 2008 Moore was convinced that the time had come for an American president who "embodies . . . the bringing together of separate worlds."[24]

Less for supporting Obama than for implying that "the moment for a woman president has passed," as a letter writer to the *New York Times* understood it, Moore's op-ed attracted charges of deficient feminism.[25] Later she defended her preference for the male candidate for the Democratic nomination over his female rival, Hillary Clinton: "I'm a feminist. But not to the exclusion of all else, and one votes as many things. If one can only vote as a woman seeking a belated registration of women in the political landscape, if as a woman one can vote only for a woman no matter who she is—one, say, who championed an immoral war—one may miss more important opportunities. . . . Certainly one can be a feminist and vote for Obama, and most feminists I know personally will and do."[26] Never a doctrinaire feminist, and ever suspicious of "group-think,"[27] she regularly creates female characters who are criticized by other, more dogmatic women. "Paper Losses" contains a parenthetical prolepsis in which Kit's neighbor rehearses the feminist principle of not blaming the other woman for one's husband's adultery and receives a round reply from Kit, who may wonder why female solidarity didn't restrain her husband's mistress from becoming involved with a married man in the first place.

Competition between women with designs on the same man crops up regularly in Moore's fiction, and its incompatibility with feminist thinking is underlined humorously in "Terrific

Mother," when Adrienne observes, "I think there's something wrong with the words *feminist* and *gets the guy* being in the same sentence."[28] In some cases (as with Benna and Eleanor in *Anagrams*) the contenders for a man's affection are friends, a problem to which Moore returns in the *New Yorker* story that preceded "Paper Losses," "The Juniper Tree."[29] Moore locates the origins of this story in a dream she had after the early death from pancreatic cancer of her filmmaker friend Nietzchka Keene, whose best-known film also went under the title *The Juniper Tree*.[30] The largely unrevised version reprinted in *The Collected Stories* is dedicated to Keene. Formally a pastiche structured around an opening narrative (friend's death), a dream (of visiting her ghost), and a flashback (to a final "real-life" visit to her house), Moore's story is driven by the unnamed first-person narrator's guilt from two sources: at failing to visit her friend, Robin, in hospital before she died, and at being involved in a fragile love affair with Robin's ex-boyfriend (also anonymous, being repeatedly designated only as "the man"). While the living Robin claimed to be "good at sharing" men (14), she took unkind satisfaction in fueling the narrator's insecurities about their common lover. The fact that the narrator was sleeping with this man on the night Robin died compounds her feeling of having betrayed Robin, and in the dream section of the story the narrator's guilty conscience is pricked by the dead Robin's "judging" smile (17).

In the third-person author's note to *The Collected Stories*, Moore explains the reverse chronology and the precedence given to the three twenty-first-century stories as follows: "The newer stories feel truer to [the author's] current interests and the older ones seem written by someone else."[31] If her "current interests" are primarily political, they are more explicitly addressed in

"Debarking" and "Paper Losses" than in "The Juniper Tree," a story that, rather than departing from earlier preoccupations, seems to reprise many of her signature interests and devices: women's conflicting resistance to maternal inheritance and need for "mother-love" (14), a faltering faith in the "magic" of language (13), and a reaching toward song or slapstick for a moment of grace. Among these familiar characteristics is the idea of incomplete belonging or being "a little out of the loop" (18). It is crystallized in the metaphor of the transplant: the narrator and her friends as "academic transplants, . . . soldiers of art stationed on a far-off base" (14), the trees drawn from fairy tales—juniper included—which Robin favored growing despite not living in "the best gardening zone" (17) for those varieties. Like almost all of Moore's fiction to date, the story creates an impression of nonindigenous, ill-adapted species (whether human or arboreal), struggling to flourish despite difficult conditions and "the witchy strangeness of the place" (16).

Moore returns to the device of transplanted characters in "Foes," by far her most overtly political work of fiction to date and one that was advertised by the London *Guardian* as an "exclusive election short story."[32] Baker McKurty and his wife, Suzy, fly into Washington, D.C., from Chicago to attend a gala dinner hosted by a magazine for which Bake writes. Residents of Michigan, they are grateful for the home-style comforts provided in their Georgetown bed and breakfast ("warm cookies . . . , tea packets . . . , snore strips," 4) and somewhat at sea among the crowds of rich and influential people whom Bake is supposed to charm out of some of their money: "They weren't really mingling. They were doing something that was more like a stiff list, a drift and sway" (2). The converted bank premises in which the dinner takes place is a sign of the times—of the 2008 banking collapse and economic downturn that contributed to the electorate's desire for a transformative new leader. But the vaulted, opulent building remains a temple to Mammon, the only difference being that business is now mixed with culture: "subtle boundaries of occasion and transaction had been given up on" (2).

Bake's distaste for the evening's commercial agenda is quick to erupt in his conversation with a lobbyist over dinner; as in "Beautiful Grade," fellow diners rapidly reveal their opposing political colors. Here the trigger for animosity is Linda Santo's disappointment that Bake, a relatively obscure biographer, is not a more famous writer. In an exchange that distills verbal irony to a caustic concentrate, Linda inquires, "'What might you have written?'" and Bake exposes the inanity of her social hedging: "'What might I have written? Or, what did I actually write?'" (3). From that point Bake veers off into self-aggrandizing fantasy, pretending to have won a Nobel Prize that received no publicity because other news stories were much higher up the running order: "'I won . . . right after 9/11. In the shadow of 9/11. Actually, I won right as the second tower was being hit'" (3).

Seven years after the September 11 terrorist strikes, then, Moore introduces them explicitly into her fiction. The reference to the attacks launches Bake and Linda into an argument about patriotism, national identity, and race, with Barack Obama— "Brocko" to Bake, "Barama" to Linda—as its focus. A pattern emerges of thrusts by Linda followed on Bake's part by increasingly shrill parries. When Linda charges the senator from Illinois with being a friend to terrorists, Bake's thoughts stray to his own terrorist friends: "balding, boring" midwesterners (recalling Nick in "Community Life") who "aged and fattened in the ordinary fashion" (3). When she implies that Obama is the beneficiary of positive racial discrimination, he cries, "You know, I never thought about it before but you're right! Being black really *is* the fastest, easiest way to get to the White House!" A veiled accusation of male chauvinism produces a mock-defensive retort about the burdens of manhood: "There's all that cash you have to spend on porno? And believe me, that's money you never get back" (4). This is one of Moore's funniest dialogues but a deep vein of hostility underlies the comedy: the more Linda addresses Bake as "my friend," the wider the gulf in sympathy and ideology that seems to open between them. With Linda's mention of "diabolical people" plotting new acts of terror, further communication becomes impossible and Bake falls silent. Paradoxically this is the prelude to sudden understanding, as Linda reveals the personal background to her fear and hatred of terrorists: that she was among those injured in the targeted crash at the Pentagon. Bake now realizes that he has been guilty of his own diabolizing, having perceived Linda's unnaturally shiny black hair, stretched complexion, talonlike fingernails, and clawlike hand as outward signs of inhumanity when in fact they are the consequences of burn wounds, hair replacement, and reconstructive surgery. Pity and admiration flood through him, but not in a saccharine conversion to amicability: for all his acknowledgment of her suffering and courage, he still has to suppress the impulse to strangle her.

If Bake and Linda are not and never could be friends, Bake and Suzy are friends as well as spouses, their relationship providing one of the most heartening models of conjugal companionship in all Moore's work to date. Past their prime in age (Bake is sixty) and sexual activity (in a deft simile Bake's penis is described as sitting "soft as a shrinking peach in his pants," 3), they are portrayed as loving allies the strength of whose union is symbolized by their tenderly joined hands bearing identical wedding rings. Moore stops short of sentimentality: there are hints of inevitable separation in death, and the story ends with a tableau of Suzy looking beautiful and otherworldly—like previous vanishing birds in Moore's fiction—as she gazes out of the taxicab window. But Suzy's assent to Bake's only half-joking request for eternal togetherness encapsulates their reciprocal kindness, and her comforting prediction that Obama will be elected president serves as a closing benediction on a par with the toasts and blessings in earlier stories:

> "Brocko is going to win. All will be well. Rest assured." . . .
> "Promise?"
> "Promise." (4)

Notes

Chapter 1—Introduction

1. Lorrie Moore, "How to Become a Writer," *New York Times Book Review,* March 3, 1985, 3, collected in *Self-Help,* by Lorrie Moore (New York: Alfred A. Knopf, 1985; London: Faber & Faber, 1998). Page references are to the Faber edition.

2. Angela Pneuman, interview with Lorrie Moore, *Believer*, October 2005, http://www.believermag.com/issues/200510/?read=interview_moore (accessed May 11, 2007).

3. Boris Kachka, "Influences: Lorrie Moore," interview with Lorrie Moore, *New York,* July 17, 2005, http://nymag.com/nymetro/arts/books/12234 (accessed May 14, 2007).

4. Don Lee, "About Lorrie Moore," interview with Lorrie Moore, *Contemporary Literary Criticism* 165 (2003): 217. The interview originally appeared in *Ploughshares* 24, nos. 2–3 (1998): 224–29.

5. The term "the boonies" is taken from Lorrie Moore, "The Jewish Hunter," in *Like Life* (New York: Alfred A. Knopf, 1990; London: Faber & Faber, 2001). Page references are to the Faber edition.

6. Interview with Lorrie Moore, *Madison Review* 23, no. 2 (2002): 50.

7. Moore, "The Jewish Hunter." The story first appeared in the *New Yorker,* November 13, 1989.

8. Pneuman, interview with Moore.

9. Moore, "How to Become a Writer," 124.

10. Pneuman, interview with Moore.

11. Ibid.

12. Lorrie Moore, *Anagrams* (New York: Alfred A. Knopf, 1986; New York: Warner Books, 1997). Page references are to the Warner Books edition.

13. Robert Frost, "The Road Not Taken" (1916).

14. Lorrie Moore, talk given in March 2000 at Baruch College, City University of New York, where Moore was Sidney Harman Writer in Residence. Video at http://www.baruch.cuny.edu/dml/engine.php?action (accessed May 14, 2007).

15. Elizabeth Gaffney, "Lorrie Moore: The Art of Fiction 167," interview with Lorrie Moore, *Contemporary Literary Criticism* 165 (2003): 239. The interview originally appeared in *Paris Review* 43, no. 158 (2001): 57–84.

16. Ibid., 241.

17. Lorrie Moore, "Unanswered Prayer," review of *Checkpoint,* by Nicholson Baker, *New York Review of Books,* November 4, 2004, 30.

18. Michael Silverblatt, interview with Lorrie Moore, KCRW *Bookworm,* July 15, 1999, http://play.rbn.com/?url=livecon/kcrw-cp/demand/bw/bw1990715Lorrie_Moore.ra (accessed June 29, 2006).

19. Pneuman, interview with Moore.

20. Lorrie Moore, *The Forgotten Helper* (New York: Kipling Press, 1987; New York: Yearling Books, 2002).

21. Pneuman, interview with Moore.

22. Lorrie Moore, ed., *The Faber Book of Contemporary Stories about Childhood* (London: Faber & Faber, 1997), xii.

23. Ibid., xi.

24. "You're Ugly, Too" was first published in the July 3, 1989, issue of the *New Yorker*. It has been reprinted in John Updike, ed., *Best American Short Stories of the Century* (Boston: Houghton Mifflin, 2000); David Remnick, ed., *Wonderful Town: New York Stories from the New Yorker* (New York: Random House, 2000); Lex Williford and Michael Martone, eds., *The Scribner Anthology of Contemporary Short Fiction: Fifty North American Stories since 1970* (New York: Scribner, 1999); and Kate Figes, ed., *The Penguin Book of International Women's Stories* (New York: Penguin Books, 1997).

25. For the publication history of "You're Ugly, Too," see note 24 above, and for that of "The Jewish Hunter," see note 7. "Two Boys" first appeared in the *Gentlemen's Quarterly* 59, no. 4 (1989): 211;

"Vissi d'Arte" in *New York Woman* and "Places to Look for Your Mind" in the *Tampa Review*.

26. The revised wording is "Alarm buzzed through her, mildly, like a tea"; Moore, "You're Ugly, Too," in *Like Life* (New York: Alfred A. Knopf; London: Faber & Faber, 2001). Page references (in this case, p. 85) are to the Faber edition.

27. Edwidge Danticat, Adam Haslett, and Amy Hempel, jurors' tribute in the 2004 Rea Award, http://www.reaaward.org/html/lorrie_moore.html (accessed May 14, 2007).

28. Juliet Fleming, "Deer in the Headlights," *Times Literary Supplement* 4987 (October 30, 1998): 27. The article was reprinted in *Contemporary Literary Criticism* 165 (2003): 220–23.

29. For positive appraisals of Moore's humor and wordplay, see, for example, Erin McGraw, "Man Walks into a Bar," *Georgia Review* 53, no. 4 (1999): 775–78; Vince Passaro, "Unlikely Stories: The Quiet Renaissance of American Short Fiction," *Harper's*, August 1999, 80–89; Michelle Brockway, "The Art of Reading Lorrie Moore," *Poets and Writers* 28, no. 5 (2000): 16–19; and Julian Barnes, "The Wise Woman," *New York Review of Books,* October 22, 1998, 15 (reprinted in *Contemporary Literary Criticism* 165 [2003]: 218–19).

30. For the tasteless joke that provides the title to "You're Ugly, Too," see Lorrie Moore, *Like Life*, 77.

31. Lorrie Moore, "Places to Look for Your Mind," in Moore, *Like Life*, 92–115, quotation on 107; Lorrie Moore, "Vissi d'Arte," in Moore, *Like Life*, 20–48.

32. Lorrie Moore, "Like Life," in Moore, *Like Life*, 149–78.

33. Moore, "Vissi d'Arte," 48.

34. Lorrie Moore, *Who Will Run the Frog Hospital?* (New York: Alfred A. Knopf, 1994; London: Faber & Faber, 1995). Page references (in this case, p. 9) are to the Faber edition.

35. See, for instance, Victoria Jenkins, "Two Teenage Girls, One Praying for 'Things to Happen,'" *Chicago Tribune Books,* October 23, 1994, 3; Valerie Miner, "Connections and Disconnections,"

Women's Review of Books 12, no. 7 (1995): 14–15; and Carole Stabile, review of *Who Will Run the Frog Hospital?* by Lorrie Moore, *Belles Lettres* 11, no. 1 (1996): 45–46.

36. Miner, "Connections and Disconnections," 15. See also Michael Griffith, "'All of Us Dislike the Laws of Nature': New Fiction in Review," *Southern Review* 31, no. 2 (1995): 365–80.

37. Lorrie Moore, "Paris," *New Yorker*, June 13, 1994, 84–92.

38. Gaffney, "Lorrie Moore," 243.

39. Pneuman, interview with Moore.

40. Lorrie Moore, ed., *The Best American Short Stories 2004* (Boston: Houghton Mifflin, 2004), xv.

41. Gaffney, "Lorrie Moore," 243.

42. Ibid.

43. These were "Willing," *New Yorker*, May 14, 1990, 39; "Community Life," *New Yorker*, September 30, 1991, 29; "Charades," *New Yorker*, April 20, 1992, 37; "Terrific Mother," *Paris Review* 34, no. 124 (1992): 90; "Dance in America," *New Yorker*, June 28, 1993, 82; "Which Is More Than I Can Say about Some People," *New Yorker*, November 8, 1993, 108; and "If Only Bert Were Here" (subsequently "Four Calling Birds, Three French Hens"), *New York Times*, December 25, 1993, A31.

44. "Beautiful Grade" was originally published in the *New Yorker*, December 25, 1995, 116; "Agnes of Iowa" in *Granta* 54 (Summer 1996): 193–208; "People Like That Are the Only People Here" in the *New Yorker*, January 27, 1997, 58–72; and "Real Estate" in the *New Yorker*, August 17, 1998, 66–74. *Harper's* carried an early version of "What You Want to Do Fine" called "Lucky Ducks" (*Harper's*, March 1998, 65–78).

45. In a *Salon* interview in 1998 Moore said that the title is "meant to refer to the Audubon book" rather than to Mary McCarthy's 1971 novel *Birds of America*, which she does not regard as a significant influence. "Moore's Better Blues," *Salon*, http://www.salon.com/books/int/1998/10/cov_27int.html (accessed April 13, 2002).

46. John Blades, "Lorrie Moore: Flipping Death the Bird," *Publishers Weekly* 245, no. 34 (1998): 31.

47. Danticat, Haslett, and Hempel, jurors' tribute.

48. Lorrie Moore, "People Like That Are the Only People Here," in *Birds of America*, by Lorrie Moore (New York: Alfred A. Knopf, 1998; London: Faber & Faber, 1999), 222. Citation from the Faber edition.

49. Moore, Baruch College talk.

50. Gaffney, "Lorrie Moore," 238.

51. The O. Henry prize winners were "Charades" (1993), "Terrific Mother" (1994), and "People Like That Are the Only People Here" (1998). Recent honors include the Rea Award (2004), the PEN/Malamud Award (2005), both for distinction in short fiction; a Cornell University Distinguished Alumni Artist Award (2004–5); and an honorary doctorate from St. Lawrence University (2004). Moore has also received a Guggenheim Fellowship, a Lannan Foundation Fellowship, a Rome Fellowship from the American Academy of Arts and Letters, a National Magazine Award for Fiction, and an Irish Times International Prize for Fiction.

52. Lorrie Moore, *The Collected Stories of Lorrie Moore* (London: Faber & Faber, 2008).

53. Moore, "Unanswered Prayer," 30.

54. Interview with Lorrie Moore, *Madison Review* 23, no. 2 (2002): 51.

55. Moore, *Best American Short Stories 2004*, xvi.

56. Ibid., xviii.

57. Moore, "Unanswered Prayer," 30.

58. Lorrie Moore, "The Juniper Tree," *New Yorker,* January 17, 2005, http://www.newyorker.com/printables/fiction/050117fi_fiction (accessed March 10, 2006).

59. Lorrie Moore, "Debarking," *New Yorker,* December 22 and 29, 2003, http://www.newyorker.com/fiction/content/?031222fi_fiction (accessed July 10, 2006); Lorrie Moore, "Paper Losses," *New Yorker,* November 6, 2006, http://www.newyorker.com/archive/2006/11/06/061106fi_fiction (accessed May 14, 2007); Lorrie Moore, "Foes," *Guardian* (London), November 1, 2008, Review

sec., 2–4 (also available online at http://www.guardian.co.uk/books/ 2008/nov/01/lorrie-moore-story [accessed December 2, 2008]).

60. Pneuman, interview with Moore.

61. Available at http://www.nchicha.com/cupofchicha/archives/ 002076.shtml (accessed May 14, 2007).

62. "Lorrie Moore Reading—a Report" (about a reading by Moore at the Hammer Museum, Los Angeles, on February 25, 2005), *The Elegant Variation: A Literary Blog*, February 28, 2005, http://marksarvas.blogs.com/elegvar/2005/02/lorrie_moore_re.html (accessed June 4, 2007); Moore, Baruch College talk.

63. Moore, *Collected Stories*, vii. Moore announced the novel's completion to an audience at the Rothermere American Institute, University of Oxford, when giving an Esmond Harmsworth lecture titled "Random Things One Can Learn from a Visiting Writer," on May 29, 2008. It is scheduled for publication by Alfred A. Knopf in September 2009 and by Faber in October 2009.

Chapter 2—*Self-Help*

1. Lorrie Moore, *Self-Help* (New York: Alfred A. Knopf, 1985; London: Faber & Faber, 1998). Page references are to the Faber edition.

2. Elizabeth Gaffney, "Lorrie Moore: The Art of Fiction 167," interview with Lorrie Moore, *Contemporary Literary Criticism* 165 (2003): 242–43.

3. Ibid., 240.

4. Ibid.

5. Angela Pneuman, interview with Lorrie Moore, *Believer*, October 2005, http://www.believermag.com/issues/2005010/?read= interview_moore, n.p. (accessed May 11, 2007).

6. Nathaniel Hawthorne, "The Haunted Mind," in *Nathaniel Hawthorne's Tales* (London: W. W. Norton, 1972), 55–58; Jay McInerney, *Bright Lights, Big City* (New York: Vintage, 1984).

7. For articles discussing various aspects of the poetics and politics of the second person, see the special issue of *Style* devoted to second-person narrative: Monika Fludernik, ed., *Style* 28, no. 3 (1994).

8. James Phelan, "*Self-Help* for Narratee and Narrative Audience: How 'I'—and 'You'—Read 'How,'" *Contemporary Literary Criticism* 165 (2003): 199–207. The article originally appeared in *Style* 28, no. 3 (1994): 350–65.

9. Ibid., 199.

10. Susan Minot, "Lust," in *Lust and Other Stories* (1989; London: Vintage, 1999), 3–17; Joyce Carol Oates, *Middle Age: A Romance* (2001; London: Fourth Estate, 2002), 1.

11. Jay McInerney, "New and Improved Lives," *New York Times*, March 24, 1985, http://www.nytimes.com/books/98/09/20/specials/moore-help.html (accessed May 9, 2007).

12. McInerney, *Bright Lights, Big City*, 166–67.

13. Sylvia Plath, "A Day in June" (1949), in *Johnny Panic and the Bible of Dreams and Other Prose Writings* (London: Faber & Faber, 1979), 247–50; Tama Janowitz, "Sun Poisoning" and "You and the Boss," in *Slaves of New York* (1986; London: Bloomsbury, 2002), 58–65 and 36–41; Pam Houston, "How to Talk to a Hunter," in *Cowboys Are My Weakness* (1992; London: Virago, 1999), 13–20.

14. Phelan, "*Self-Help* for Narratee and Narrative Audience," 204.

15. Explicit references to women losing their minds occur in "How to Be an Other Woman" (12) and "To Fill" (134). In "How to Become a Writer" there is a related suggestion, that Francie is "losing . . . [her] balance" (125).

16. The idea of the empty house as a metaphor for barrenness features in Moore's later story "You're Ugly, Too," in *Like Life* (New York: Alfred A. Knopf, 1990; London: Faber & Faber, 2001). Page references (in this case, p. 90) are to the Faber edition. Moore comments on the difficulty of writing satisfactory short stories about abortion in "Patios & Poolsides," *New York Review of Books*, November 16, 2000, http://www.nybooks.com/articles/13903 (accessed February 6, 2008).

17. The term comes from Monika Fludernik, "Second-Person Narrative as a Test Case for Narratology: The Limits of Realism," *Style* 28, no. 3 (1994): 462.

18. Phelan, "*Self-Help* for Narratee and Narrative Audience," 203.

19. The "you"-character in "The Kid's Guide to Divorce" is never named or assigned a gender, but certain details suggest (without conclusively designating) that she is female: her "slippers and robe" (49), her physical intimacy with her mother (50, 51), her pretense of reading a magazine (52), and the fact that the friend she mentions is a girl (52).

20. For a discussion of "the politics of narrative person," see Brian Richardson, "I Etcetera: On the Poetics and Ideology of Multi-personed Narratives," *Style* 28, no. 3 (1994): 312–28; and Keith Green and Jill LeBihan, "The Speaking Object: Daphne Marlatt's Pronouns and Lesbian Poetics," *Style* 28, no. 3 (1994): 432–44.

21. Fludernik, "Second-Person Narrative," 469.

Chapter 3—*Anagrams*

1. Elizabeth Gaffney, "Lorrie Moore: The Art of Fiction 167," interview with Lorrie Moore, *Contemporary Literary Criticism* 165 (2003): 239.

2. Lorrie Moore, *The Collected Stories of Lorrie Moore* (London: Faber & Faber, 2008), viii.

3. Gaffney, "Lorrie Moore," 238.

4. Ibid.

5. Barbara Lovenheim, telephone interview with Lorrie Moore, *New York Times,* November 2, 1986, http://www.nytimes.com/books/98/09/20/specials/moore-anagrams.html (accessed September 5, 2007).

6. Karen Weekes, "Postmodernism in Women's Short Story Cycles: Lorrie Moore's *Anagrams,*" in *The Postmodern Short Story: Forms and Issues,* ed. Farhat Iftekharrudin, Joseph Boyden, Mary Rohrberger, and Jaie Claudet (Westport, Conn.: Praeger, 2003), 95.

7. Ibid., 97.

8. Maggie Dunn and Ann Morris, *The Composite Novel: The Short Story Cycle in Transition* (New York: Twayne, 1995); Margot

Kelley, "Gender and Genre: The Case of the Novel-in-Stories," in *American Short Story Writers: A Collection of Critical Essays,* ed. Julie Brown (New York: Garland, 1995).

9. Kelley, "Gender and Genre"; Ellen G. Friedman and Miriam Fuchs, "Contexts and Continuities: An Introduction to Women's Experimental Fiction in English," in *Breaking the Sequence: Women's Experimental Fiction,* ed. Ellen G. Friedman and Miriam Fuchs (Princeton: Princeton University Press, 1989).

10. Carol Anshaw, *Aquamarine* (1992; London: Virago, 1993).

11. Philip Roth, *The Counterlife* (New York: Farrar, Straus, & Giroux, 1986).

12. Lorrie Moore, *Anagrams* (1986; New York: Warner Books, 1997), 3.

13. Lovenheim, interview with Moore.

14. See chapter 1, note 24, for the publication history of "You're Ugly, Too." "Real Estate" first appeared in the August 17, 1998, *New Yorker* before being included in Lorrie Moore, *Birds of America* (New York: Alfred A. Knopf, 1998; London: Faber & Faber, 1999), 177–221. Page references are to the Faber edition.

15. Susan Sontag, *Illness as Metaphor* (New York: Farrar, Straus, & Giroux, 1978), 44, 14, 13.

16. Sontag, *Illness as Metaphor,* 9, 68, 67.

17. Gaffney, "Lorrie Moore," 242.

18. Debra Shostak, *Philip Roth—Countertexts, Counterlives* (Columbia: University of South Carolina Press, 2004).

19. Ibid., 6.

20. Carol Hill, "Sestinas and Wisecracks," *New York Times Book Review,* November 2, 1986, http://www.nytimes.com/books/98/09/20/specials/Moore-anagrams.html (accessed September 5, 2007).

21. Michiko Kakutani, "Jokers Wild," *New York Times Book Review,* October 18, 1986. Accessed online at http://www.nytimes.com (September 5, 2007).

22. Kakutani quotes the passage without analysis in a list of "terrible jokes and puns"; ibid.

23. Gaffney, "Lorrie Moore," 238.

24. Moore applies this term to *Ideas of Heaven* by Joan Silber in "Love's Wreckage," *New York Review of Books,* August 11, 2005, http://www.nybooks.com/articles/18172 (accessed February 6, 2008).

25. Weekes, "Postmodernism in Women's Short Story Cycles," 98.

Chapter 4—*Like Life*

1. Don Lee, "About Lorrie Moore," interview with Lorrie Moore, *Contemporary Literary Criticism* 165 (2003): 217.

2. Carol Iannone, "Post-Counterculture Tristesse," *Commentary* 83, no. 2 (1987): 57–61; John W. Aldridge, *Talents and Technicians: Literary Chic and the New Assembly-Line Fiction* (New York: Charles Scribner's Sons, 1992), 106.

3. Lorrie Moore, talk given in March 2000 at Baruch College, City University of New York, where Moore was Sidney Harman Writer in Residence. Video at http://www.baruch.cuny.edu/dml/engine.php?action (accessed May 14, 2007).

4. Lorrie Moore, *The Forgotten Helper* (New York: Kipling Press, 1987; New York: Yearling Books, 2002).

5. Lorrie Moore, *Like Life* (New York: Alfred A. Knopf, 1990; London: Faber & Faber, 2001). Page references are to the Faber edition.

6. Stephen McCauley, "Love Is Like a Truck on the Interstate," *New York Times,* May 20, 1990, http://www.nytimes.com/books/98/09/20/specials/moore-life.html (accessed December 2, 2008).

7. Janet R. Raiffa, entry on Moore in *The Columbia Companion to the Twentieth-Century American Short Story,* ed. Blanche H. Gelfant (New York: Columbia University Press, 2000), 386.

8. Elizabeth Gaffney, "Lorrie Moore: The Art of Fiction 167," interview with Lorrie Moore, *Contemporary Literary Criticism* 165 (2003): 244.

9. See, for example, Peter Brooker, *New York Fictions: Modernity, Postmodernism, the New Modern* (London: Longman, 1996), 7.

10. Susan Minot, "City Night" and "Sparks," both in *Lust & Other Stories* (Boston: Houghton Mifflin, 1989).

11. Robert Chodat, "Jokes, Fiction, and Lorrie Moore," *Twentieth-Century Literature* 52, no. 1 (2006): 46, 50.

12. Ibid., 58.

13. Lorrie Moore, "Bioperversity," *New Yorker,* May 19, 2003, http://www.newyorker.com/archive/2003/05/19/030519crbo_books2?printable=true (accessed February 6, 2008).

14. Cf. Mamie in Moore, "Like Life," 178.

15. Mamie's verdict on Rudy's impression of Bob Dylan; Moore, "Like Life," 158.

16. Juliet Fleming, "Deer in the Headlights," *Times Literary Supplement* 4987 (October 30, 1998): 27; Michelle Brockway, "The Art of Reading Lorrie Moore," *Poets and Writers* 28, no. 5 (2000): 16–19; both reprinted in *Contemporary Literary Criticism* 165 (2003): 223–26 and 234–36, respectively.

Chapter 5—*Who Will Run the Frog Hospital?*

1. Moore was awarded a Guggenheim Fellowship in 1991 and a Rome Fellowship from the American Academy of Arts and Letters in 1992. She received O. Henry prizes for two *New Yorker* stories that would later be collected in her *Birds of America*: "Charades" and "Terrific Mother."

2. Lorrie Moore, "Voters in Wonderland," *New York Times,* November 3, 1992, A19.

3. Lorrie Moore, *Who Will Run the Frog Hospital?* (New York: Alfred A. Knopf, 1994; London: Faber & Faber, 1995). Page references are to the Faber edition.

4. Jean Baudrillard, *America,* trans. Chris Turner (London: Verso, 1988), 104.

5. Ibid., 29.

6. Caryn James, "I Feel His Lack of Love for Me," *New York Times,* October 9, 1994, http://www.nytimes.com/books/98/09/20/specials/moore-frog.html (accessed December 2, 2008).

7. Lorrie Moore, "Home Truths," review of *The Early Stories, 1953–1975*, by John Updike, *New York Review of Books*, November 20, 2003, http://www.nybooks.com/articles/16794 (accessed February 6, 2008).

8. Lorrie Moore, "Paris," *New Yorker*, June 13, 1994, 84–92.

9. Lorrie Moore, interview with the author, June 2008.

10. Victoria Jenkins, "Two Teenage Girls, One Praying for 'Things to Happen,'" *Contemporary Literary Criticism* 165 (2003): 207. Originally published in *Chicago Tribune Books*, October 23, 1994, 3.

11. Carole Stabile, review of *Who Will Run the Frog Hospital?* by Lorrie Moore, *Contemporary Literary Criticism* 165 (2003): 212–13. Originally published in *Belles Lettres* 11, no. 1 (1996): 45–46.

12. Tom Shone, "Smart-Aleck Scenes," *Contemporary Literary Criticism* 165 (2003): 208. Originally published in *Times Literary Supplement* 4479 (November 4, 1994): 22.

13. Griffith, "'All of Us Dislike the Laws of Nature': New Fiction in Review," *Contemporary Literary Criticism* 165 (2003): 210. Originally published in *Southern Review* 31, no. 2 (1995): 365–80.

14. Monica Fagan, "Choirs and Split Voices: Female Identity Construction in Lorrie Moore's *Who Will Run the Frog Hospital?*" *College Literature* 33, no. 2 (2006): 52–69, http://findarticles.com/p/articles/mi_qa3709/is_200604/ai_n17184343/print (accessed September 3, 2007).

15. Valerie Miner, "Connections and Disconnections," *Contemporary Literary Criticism* 165 (2003): 211. Originally published in *Women's Review of Books* 12, no. 7 (1995): 14–15.

16. John Berger, *Ways of Seeing* (Harmondsworth: Penguin, 1972).

17. Ibid., 47.

18. Fagan, "Choirs and Split Voices."

19. Ted Cohen, *Jokes: Philosophical Thoughts on Joking Matters* (Chicago: University of Chicago Press, 1999), 29.

20. Lorrie Moore, "Made in the USA," *New York Review of Books*, August 12, 1999, http://www.nybooks.com/articles/402 (accessed June 2, 2008).

21. Interview with Lorrie Moore, *Madison Review* 23, no. 2 (2002): 50.

22. Griffith, "'All of Us Dislike the Laws of Nature.'"

23. David C. Rubin, ed., *Remembering Our Past: Studies in Autobiographical Memory* (1995; Cambridge: Cambridge University Press, 1999), 9.

24. Ibid., 4.

25. Miner, "Connections and Disconnections," 211.

Chapter 6—*Birds of America*

1. Lorrie Moore, *Birds of America* (New York: Alfred A. Knopf, 1998; London: Faber & Faber, 1998). References in the text are to the Faber edition. The collection entered the *New York Times* best-seller list on October 11, 1998, in fourteenth place, slipped to fifteenth position on October 18, and was ranked fourteenth again on October 25.

2. Don Lee, "About Lorrie Moore," interview with Lorrie Moore, *Contemporary Literary Criticism* 165 (2003): 218.

3. James McManus, "The Unbearable Lightness of Being," *New York Times,* September 20, 1998, http://www.nytimes.com/books/98/09/20/reviews/980920.20mcmanut.html (accessed October 31, 2008).

4. Julian Barnes, "The Wise Woman," *Contemporary Literary Criticism* 165 (2003): 219 (originally published in *New York Review of Books,* October 22, 1998, 15); Erin McGraw, "Man Walks into a Bar," *Contemporary Literary Criticism* 165 (2003): 225 (originally published in *Georgia Review* 53, no. 4 (1999): 775–78); James Urquhart, "Dysfunctional Sitcoms," *Contemporary Literary Criticism* 165 (2003): 227 (originally published in *New Statesman,* January 8, 1999, 58); Michael Frank, "Fiction in Review," *Contemporary Literary Criticism* 165 (2003): 228 (originally published in *Yale Review* 87, no. 2 (1999): 157–74).

5. Michiko Kakutani, "'Birds of America': And What Have They Done with Their Lives?" *New York Times,* September 11, 1998, http://www.nytimes.com/books/98/09/06/daily/birds-book-review.html (accessed November 2, 2008).

6. McManus, "Unbearable Lightness of Being."

7. Elizabeth Gaffney, "Lorrie Moore: The Art of Fiction 167," interview with Lorrie Moore, *Contemporary Literary Criticism* 165 (2003): 237.

8. Lorrie Moore, "Chop-Suey Xmas," *New Yorker,* December 22, 1997, http://www.newyorker.com/archive/1997/12/22/1997 _12_22_087_TNY_CARDS_00 (accessed February 6, 2008).

9. Richard Ford, ed., *New Granta Book of the American Short Story* (London: Granta, 2007).

10. Katharine Young, "Narrative Embodiments: Enclaves of the Self in the Realm of Medicine," in *Texts of Identity,* ed. John Shotter and Kenneth J. Gergen (London: Sage, 1989), 153.

11. Angela Pneuman, interview with Lorrie Moore, *Believer*, October 2005, http://www.believermag.com/issues/2005010/?read= interview_moore, n.p. (accessed May 11, 2007).

12. Amy Bloom, "A Blind Man Can See How Much I Love You," in *A Blind Man Can See How Much I Love You* (London: Picador, 2000), 1–29. For a discussion of medical waiting rooms in American literature, see Laura Tanner, "Bodies in Waiting: Representations of Medical Waiting Rooms in Contemporary American Fiction," *American Literary History* 14, no. 1 (2002): 115–30.

13. See Moore's comments on Suzanne Marrs's biography of Eudora Welty in Lorrie Moore, "A Pondered Life," *New York Review of Books,* September 21, 2006, http://www.nybooks.com/ articles/19299 (accessed September 29, 2008).

14 "Four Calling Birds, Three French Hens" was first published as "If Only Bert Were Here," *New York Times,* December 25, 1993, A31.

15. See Olena's references to literary theory on page 62 of "Community Life."

16. McManus, "Unbearable Lightness of Being."

17. The center is a fictionalized version of Bellagio, the Rockefeller Foundation's writers' colony on Lake Como.

18. Michael Silverblatt, interview with Lorrie Moore, KCRW *Bookworm,* July 15, 1999, http://play.rbn.com/?url=livecon/ kcrw-cp/demand/bw/bw1990715Lorrie_Moore.ra (accessed June 29, 2006).

19. Lorrie Moore, "What Is Seized," in Moore, *Self-Help* (1985; London: Faber & Faber, 1987), 32.

20. Lorrie Moore, *Who Will Run the Frog Hospital?* (1994; London: Faber & Faber, 1995), 121.

21. See Deborah Clarke, 'Domesticating the Car: Women's Road Trips,' *Studies in American Fiction* 32, no. 1 (2004): 101–29.

22. Lorrie Moore, "Lucky Ducks," *Harper's,* March 1998, 65–88.

23. Robert Bellah, Richard Madsen, William M. Sullivan, Ann Swidler, and Steven M. Tipton, *Habits of the Heart: Middle America Observed* (1985; London: Hutchinson, 1988), vi.

24. Frank, "Fiction in Review," 228.

25. Urquhart, "Dysfunctional Sitcoms," 227.

26. Anita Brookner, "The Way We Live Now," *Contemporary Literary Criticism* 165 (2003): 220. Originally published in *Spectator*, October 24, 1998, 46–47.

Chapter 7—Other Works

1. Lorrie Moore, "Debarking," *New Yorker,* December 22 and 29, 2003, http://www.newyorker.com/fiction/content/?031222fi _fiction (accessed October 7, 2006). Reprinted with minor emendations in Moore, *The Collected Stories of Lorrie Moore* (London: Faber & Faber, 2008), 23–54.

2. Ulrich Baer, ed., *110 Stories: New York Writes after September 11* (New York: New York University Press, 2002); Jay McInerney, "Brightness Falls," *Guardian,* September 15, 2001, http://www .guardian.co.uk/books/2001/sep/15/september11.usa1 (accessed November 2, 2008).

3. Don DeLillo, "In the Ruins of the Future," *Guardian,* December 22, 2001, http://www.guardian.co.uk/books/2001/dec/22/ fiction.dondelillo (accessed November 2, 2008).

4. Interview with Lorrie Moore, *Madison Review* 23, no. 2 (2002): 51.

5. Lorrie Moore, "The Awkward Age," *New York Review of Books,* September 27, 2007, 56.

6. Ibid.

7. George W. Bush, victory speech delivered aboard the returning aircraft carrier USS *Abraham Lincoln*, May 1, 2003.

8. In a question-and-answer session at the University of Central Florida in April 2004, Moore acknowledged her subconscious tendency to keep creating, "accidentally," characters who work at historical societies; http://www.nchicha.com/cupofchicha/archives/002076shtml (accessed May 14, 2007).

9. Interview with Lorrie Moore, *Madison Review* 23, no. 2 (2002): 50.

10. Lorrie Moore, interview with the author, June 2008.

11. Lorrie Moore, "Paper Losses," *New Yorker*, November 6, 2006, http://www.newyorker.com/archive/2006/11/06/061106fi_fiction (accessed May 14, 2007); reprinted with revisions in Moore, *Collected Stories*, 3–12.

12. Lorrie Moore, "The Modern Elizabethan," *New York Times*, April 23, 2006, http://www.nytimes.com/2006/04/23/opinion/23moorehtml?_r=l&sq=lorriemoore& (accessed February 6, 2008); Lorrie Moore, "Home Truths," review of *The Early Stories, 1953–1975*, by John Updike, *New York Review of Books*, November 20, 2003, http://www.nybooks.com/articles/16794 (accessed February 6, 2008).

13. Lorrie Moore, "Artship," *New York Review of Books*, January 17, 2002, http://www.nybooks.com/articles/15112 (accessed February 6, 2008).

14. Lorrie Moore, *Anagrams* (1986; New York: Warner Books, 1997), 208.

15. Moore, "Patios & Poolsides," *New York Review of Books*, November 16, 2000, http://www.nybooks.com/articles/13903 (accessed February 6, 2008).

16. Interview with Lorrie Moore, *Madison Review* 23, no. 2 (2002): 50–51.

17. Lorrie Moore, "Last Year's Role Model," *New York Times*, January 13, 2008, http://www.nytimes.com/2008/01/13/opinion/13moore.html (accessed December 2, 2008).

18. Moore, interview with the author.

19. Angela Pneuman, interview with Lorrie Moore, *Believer*, October 2005, http://www.believermag.com/issues/2005010/?read=interview_moore, n.p. (accessed May 11, 2007).

20. Lorrie Moore, "The Odd Women," *New York Review of Books*, April 13, 2000, http://www.nybooks.com/articles/156 (accessed February 6, 2008).

21. Lorrie Moore, "A Pondered Life," *New York Review of Books*, September 21, 2006, http://www.nybooks.com/articles/19299 (accessed September 29, 2008); Moore, "The Odd Women."

22. Moore, "Home Truths."

23. Lorrie Moore, "Chop-Suey Xmas," *New Yorker*, December 22, 1997, 87.

24. Moore, "Last Year's Role Model."

25. Letters, "Snapshots of a Campaign in Flux," *New York Times*, January 18, 2008, http://www.nytimes.com/2008/01/18/opinion/l18elect.html (accessed February 6, 2008).

26. Moore, interview with the author.

27. Moore, "The Odd Women."

28. Lorrie Moore, "Terrific Mother," in Moore, *Birds of America* (1998; London: Faber & Faber, 1998), 278.

29. Lorrie Moore, "The Juniper Tree," *New Yorker*, January 17, 2005, http://www.newyorker.com/printables/fiction/050117fi_fiction (accessed March 10, 2006). Reprinted with minor emendations in Moore, *Collected Stories*, 13–22; page references are to this version.

30. Moore, interview with the author.

31. Moore, *Collected Stories*, vii.

32. *Guardian* (London), November 1, 2008, Review sec., 1, announcing Lorrie Moore, "Foes," ibid., Review sec., 2–4. References are hereafter made parenthetically in text.

Selected Bibliography

Works by Lorrie Moore

Fiction as Author

Self-Help. New York: Alfred A. Knopf, 1985; London: Faber & Faber, 1985.

Anagrams. New York: Alfred A. Knopf, 1986; London: Faber & Faber, 1987.

The Forgotten Helper. New York: Kipling Press, 1987.

Like Life. New York: Alfred A. Knopf, 1990; London: Faber & Faber, 1990.

Who Will Run the Frog Hospital? New York: Alfred A. Knopf, 1994; London: Faber & Faber, 1994.

Birds of America. New York: Alfred A. Knopf, 1998; London: Faber & Faber, 1998.

The Collected Stories of Lorrie Moore. London: Faber & Faber, 2008.

"Foes," *Guardian* (London), November 1, 2008, Review sec., 2–4. Also available online at http://www.guardian.co.uk/books/2008/nov/01/lorrie-moore-story (accessed December 2, 2008).

Fiction as Editor

The Faber Book of Contemporary Stories about Childhood. London: Faber & Faber, 1997.

The Best American Short Stories 2004. Selected by Lorrie Moore with Katrina Kenison, with an introduction by Lorrie Moore. Boston: Houghton Mifflin, 2004.

Selected Nonfiction

"How Humans Got Flippers and Beaks." Review of *Galapagos,* by Kurt Vonnegut. *New York Times,* October 6, 1985. http://www.nytimes.com/books/97/09/28/lifetimes/vonnegut-galapagos.html (accessed December 2, 2008).

"Onward and Upward with the Shelmikedmu." Review of *Krippen-dorf's Tribe,* by Frank Parkin. *New York Times,* March 2, 1986. Accessed online at http://www.nytimes.com (October 31, 2008).

"Trashing Women, Trashing Books." *New York Times,* December 5, 1990. http://www.nytimes.com/books/98/09/20/specials/moore-trashing.html (accessed September 5, 2007). Opinion on the controversy surrounding *American Psycho,* by Bret Easton Ellis.

"Look for a Writer and Find a Terrorist." Review of *Mao II,* by Don DeLillo. *New York Times,* June 9, 1991. http://www.nytimes.com/books/97/03/16/lifetimes/del-r-mao.html (accessed November 2, 2007).

"Every Wife's Nightmare." Review of *The Robber Bride,* by Margaret Atwood. *New York Times,* October 31, 1993. http://www.nytimes.com/books/98/09/20/specials/moore-atwood.html (accessed September 5, 2007).

"Chop-Suey Christmas." *New Yorker,* December 22, 1997. http://www.newyorker.com/archive/1997/12/22/1997_12_22_087_TNY_CARDS_00 (accessed February 6, 2008). Family anecdote.

"A House Divided." Review of *Park City: New and Selected Stories,* by Ann Beattie. *New York Times,* June 28, 1998. http://www.nytimes.com/books/98/06/28/reviews/980628.28moor.html (accessed October 31, 2008).

"Best Love Song; Two Girls and a Guy." *New York Times,* April 18, 1999. http://www.nytimes.com/library/magazine/millennium/m1/moore.html (accessed December 2, 2008). Seriocomic search for the best love song of the millennium.

"Made in the USA." Review of *Broke Heart Blues,* by Joyce Carol Oates. *New York Review of Books,* August 12, 1999. http://www.nybooks.com/articles/402 (accessed June 2, 2008).

"I'll Cut My Throat Another Day." Review of *Selected Letters of Dawn Powell, 1913–1965,* edited by Tim Page. *New York Times,* November 7, 1999. http://www.nytimes.com/books/99/11/07/reviews/991107.07mooret.html (accessed December 2, 2008).

"The Odd Women." Review of *Passionate Minds: Women Rewriting the World*, by Claudia Roth Pierpont. *New York Review of Books*, April 13, 2000. http://www.nybooks.com/articles/156 (accessed February 6, 2008).

"The Wrath of Athena." Review of *The Human Stain*, by Philip Roth. *New York Times*, May 7, 2000. http://www.nytimes.com/books/00/05/07/reviews/000507.07mooret.html (accessed December 2, 2008).

"Patios & Poolsides." Review of *Sam the Cat and Other Stories*, by Matthew Klam. *New York Review of Books*, November 16, 2000. http://www.nybooks.com/articles/13903 (accessed February 6, 2008).

"The Lives They Lived: 01–07–01: Frederic Cassidy, b. 1907; A Man of Many Words." *New York Times*, January 7, 2001. http://www.nytimes.com/library/magazine/home/20010107 magcassidy.html (accessed December 2, 2008). Obituary of a distinguished linguistic historian, Moore's colleague at the University of Wisconsin at Madison.

"Artship." Review of *Hateship, Friendship, Courtship, Loveship, Marriage*, by Alice Munro. *New York Review of Books*, January 17, 2002. http://www.nybooks.com/articles/15112 (accessed February 6, 2008).

"Bioperversity." Review of *Oryx and Crake*, by Margaret Atwood. *New Yorker*, May 19, 2003. http://www.newyorker.com/archive/2003/05/19/030519crbo_books2 (accessed December 2, 2008).

"Home Truths." Review of *The Early Stories, 1953–1975*, by John Updike. *New York Review of Books*, November 20, 2003. http://www.nybooks.com/articles/16794 (accessed February 6, 2008).

"Unanswered Prayer." Review of *Checkpoint*, by Nicholson Baker. *New York Review of Books*, November 4, 2004, 30.

"Love's Wreckage." Review of *Ideas of Heaven*, by Joan Silber. *New York Review of Books*, August 11, 2005. http://www.nybooks.com/articles/18172 (accessed September 29, 2008).

"The Modern Elizabethan." *New York Times*, April 23, 2006. http://www.nytimes.com/2006/04/23/opinion/23moore.html

(accessed December 2, 2008). Short essay on Shakespeare, concentrating on *Romeo and Juliet* and *A Midsummer Night's Dream*.

"A Pondered Life." Review of two biographies of Eudora Welty and four new editions of Welty's work. *New York Review of Books*, September 21, 2006. http://www.nybooks.com/articles/19299 (accessed September 29, 2008).

"Theater in Review." Review of John Doyle's Broadway production of *Sweeney Todd*. *Yale Review* 95 (January 2007): 197–202.

"The Awkward Age." Review of *Someday This Pain Will Be Useful to You*, by Peter Cameron. *New York Review of Books*, September 27, 2007, 53–56.

"Last Year's Role Model." *New York Times*, January 13, 2008. http://www.nytimes.com/2008/01/13/opinion/13moore.html (accessed December 2, 2008). Op-ed on 2008 presidential primaries.

Works about Lorrie Moore

Academic Articles and Chapters in Books

Aldridge, John W. "Anguish as a Second Language (David Leavitt, Lorrie Moore)." In *Talents and Technicians: Literary Chic and the New Assembly-Line Fiction*, 101–13. New York: Charles Scribner's Sons, 1992. Commends Moore's fiction for its sensitivity, style, and technique and compares her work favorably with that of her peers.

Chodat, Robert. "Jokes, Fiction, and Lorrie Moore." *Twentieth Century Literature* 52, no. 1 (2006): 42–60. An analysis of the thematic relevance and reflexive qualities of Moore's jokes, focusing on "You're Ugly, Too."

Fagan, Monica. "Choirs and Split Voices: Female Identity Construction in Lorrie Moore's *Who Will Run the Frog Hospital?*" *College Literature* 33, no. 2 (2006): 52–69. Traces the development of the friendship between Berie and Sils and argues that the loss of intimacy with Sils is damaging to Berie's mature sense of identity.

Hornby, Nick. "The *New Yorker* Short Story." In *Contemporary American Fiction*, 1–27. London: Vision Press, 1992. Discusses Moore's portraits of urban life in *Self-Help*, *Anagrams*, and *Like Life*.

Iannone, Carol. "Post-Counterculture Tristesse." *Commentary* 83, no. 2 (1987): 57–61. Identifies Moore's work as representative of a jaundiced and self-absorbed mind-set in late-twentieth-century America.

Phelan, James. "*Self-Help* for Narratee and Narrative Audience: How 'I'—and 'You'—Read 'How.'" *Style* 28, no. 3 (1994): 350–65. Reprinted in *Contemporary Literary Criticism* 165 (2003): 199–207. Analyses the shifting uses of second-person reference and address in Moore's first story collection, taking "How" as a case study.

Raiffa, Janet R. "Lorrie Moore." In *The Columbia Companion to the Twentieth-Century American Short Story*, edited by Blanche H. Gelfant, 384–90. New York: Columbia University Press, 2000. Raiffa charts Moore's development to a mature style, perhaps underestimating the depth of the early work and overstating the change of mood in *Birds of America*.

Tanner, Laura E. "Bodies in Waiting: Representations of Medical Waiting Rooms in Contemporary American Fiction." *American Literary History* 14, no. 1 (2002): 115–30. Discusses the significance of the hospital waiting room in "People Like That Are the Only People Here" in the context of a wider analysis.

Weekes, Karen. "Identity in the Short Story Cycles of Lorrie Moore." *Journal of the Short Story in English* 39 (Fall 2002): 109–22. Classifies *Self-Help*, *Anagrams*, and *Birds of America* as short-story cycles and discusses the form's suitability for representing gendered identities.

———. "Postmodernism in Women's Short Story Cycles: Lorrie Moore's *Anagrams*." In *The Postmodern Short Story: Forms and Issues*, edited by Farhat Iftekharrudin, Joseph Boyden, Mary Rohrberger, and Jaie Claudet, 94–106. Westport, Conn.: Praeger, 2003. A detailed reading of *Anagrams* as a short-story cycle, arguing that this form is particularly well suited to the chronicling of contemporary women's fragmented lives.

Selected Reviews

Barnes, Julian. "The Wise Woman." *New York Review of Books,* October 22, 1998, 15. Reprinted in *Contemporary Literary Criticism* 165 (2003): 218–19. Barnes emphasizes the seriousness underneath the wit and humor in *Birds of America.*

Blyth, Catherine. "A Child's-Eye View." *Times Literary Supplement* 4894 (January 27, 1997): 20. A tribute to Moore's sensitive anthologizing of narratives of childhood in *The Faber Book of Contemporary Stories about Childhood.*

Brockway, Michelle. "The Art of Reading Lorrie Moore." *Poets and Writers* 28, no. 5 (2000): 16–19. Reprinted in *Contemporary Literary Criticism* 165 (2003): 234–36. Praises Moore's verbal dexterity and the links between humor and deep feeling in her fiction.

Dunmore, Helen. "When the Mask Slips." *Financial Times*, May 23, 2008. High praise for *The Collected Stories* and Moore's "verve and temerity" as a short-story writer.

Fleming, Juliet. "Deer in the Headlights." *Times Literary Supplement* 4987 (October 30, 1998): 27. Reprinted in *Contemporary Literary Criticism* 165 (2003): 220–23. Largely negative appraisal of Moore's language games.

Frank, Michael. "Fiction in Review." *Yale Review* 87, no. 2 (1999): 157–74. Reprinted in *Contemporary Literary Criticism* 165 (2003): 227–31. Frank salutes the seriousness of *Birds of America* and notes the collection's interest in migrant characters.

Hill, Carol. "Sestinas and Wisecracks." *New York Times,* November 2, 1986. http://www.nytimes.com/books/98/09/20/specials/moore-anagrams.html (accessed September 5, 2007). Finds the character of Benna the redeeming feature in *Anagrams.*

James, Caryn. "I Feel His Lack of Love for Me." *New York Times,* October 9, 1994. http://www.nytimes.com/books/98/09/20/specials/moore-frog.html (accessed December 2, 2008). A positive evaluation of *Who Will Run the Frog Hospital?*

Kakutani, Michiko. "'Birds of America': And What Have They Done with Their Lives?" *New York Times*, September 11, 1998. http://www.nytimes.com/books/98/09/06/daily/birds-book-review.html (accessed December 2, 2008). Admiring review of "Ms. Moore's resonant new collection."

———. "Jokers Wild." *New York Times*, October 18, 1986. Accessed online at http://www.nytimes.com (September 5, 2007). Kakutani acknowledges the cleverness of *Anagrams* but finds it glib and dispiriting.

———. "Observations on Failures in Passion and Intimacy." *New York Times*, June 8, 1990. Accessed online at http://www.nytimes.com (October 31, 2008). Compares *Like Life* favorably with earlier work.

Kelly, Alison. "Welcome to America." *Times Literary Supplement*, May 2, 2008. A review essay based on *The Collected Stories* that discusses the political themes and national portraiture throughout Moore's work.

Mars-Jones, Adam. "Moore's Almanac of America." *Observer*, May 11, 2008. http://books.guardian.co.uk/reviews/generalfiction/0,,2279295,00.html (accessed May 14, 2008). A provocative but superficial attack on *The Collected Stories*.

McCauley, Stephen. "Love Is Like a Truck on the Interstate." *New York Times*, May 20, 1990. http://www.nytimes.com/books/98/09/20/specials/moore-life.html (accessed December 2, 2008). In contrast to most critics, McCauley finds the tone of *Like Life* broadly affirmative.

McGraw, Erin. "Man Walks into Bar." *Georgia Review* 53, no. 4 (1999): 775–78. Reprinted in *Contemporary Literary Criticism* 165 (2003): 223–26. McGraw rates Moore highly among humorous writers for the truthfulness of her comedy.

McInerney, Jay. "New and Improved Lives." *New York Times*, March 24, 1985. http://www.nytimes.com/books/98/09/20/specials/moore-help.html (accessed May 9, 2007). In this review of *Self-Help*, McInerney identifies Moore's promising talent.

McManus, James. "The Unbearable Lightness of Being." *New York Times,* September 20, 1998. http://www.nytimes.com/books/98/09/20/reviews/980920.20mcmanut.html (accessed October 31, 2008). The review that "emphatically" categorizes *Birds of America* as "a cancer book."

Miner, Valerie. "Connections and Disconnections." *Women's Review of Books* 12, no. 7 (1995): 14–15. Reprinted in *Contemporary Literary Criticism* 165 (2003): 211–12. Miner takes the view that, for all its stylistic merits, *Who Will Run the Frog Hospital?* does not make a formally satisfying novel.

Passaro, Vince. "Unlikely Stories: The Quiet Renaissance of American Short Fiction." *Harper's,* August 1999, 80–89. Passaro situates Moore's work within a late-twentieth-century regeneration of the American short story.

Tayler, Christopher. "Canonical Babbling." *Guardian,* May 16, 2008, 16. Tayler admires *The Collected Stories* but repeats the widespread view that the later fiction is more successful than the early work.

Turner, Jenny. "Angry Duck." *London Review of Books,* June 5, 2008. http://www.lrb.co.uk/v30/n11/print/turn03_.html (accessed June 9, 2008). Turner returns to Moore thirty years after first reading and reaches a more sympathetic view.

Whitworth, John. "He Wouldn't A-Wooing Go." *Spectator* 273, no. 8679 (November 12, 1994): 40. Whitworth admires certain aspects of *Who Will Run the Frog Hospital?* but implies that Moore writes mainly for a female audience.

Selected Interviews

Blades, John. "Lorrie Moore: Flipping Death the Bird." *Publishers Weekly* 245, no. 34 (1998): 31. Overview of Moore's literary career with insights into how the fiction relates to her life.

Brockes, Emma. "Lorrie Moore: A Life in Books." *Guardian* (London), June 7, 2008, 12–13. Contains some intimate glimpses of Moore's character and personal life and how these inform her writing.

Gaffney, Elizabeth. "Lorrie Moore: The Art of Fiction 167." *Paris Review* 43, no. 158 (2001): 57–84. Reprinted in *Contemporary Literary Criticism* 165 (2003): 236–45. A wide-ranging conversation about Moore's personal experiences and literary development.

Garner, Dwight. "Moore's Better Blues." *Salon,* April 13, 2002. http://www.salon.com/books/int/1998/10/cov_27int.html (accessed October 31, 2008). Interview focusing on *Birds of America.*

Lee, Don. "About Lorrie Moore: A Profile." *Ploughshares* 24, nos. 2–3 (1998): 224–29. Reprinted in *Contemporary Literary Criticism* 165 (2003): 216–18. A sketch of Moore's life and works up to and including *Birds of America.*

Index